The Atlantic Slave Trade

An Enthralling Overview of European Colonization and Slavery in the New World

© Copyright 2024 - All rights reserved.

The content contained within this book may not be reproduced, duplicated, or transmitted without direct written permission from the author or the publisher.

Under no circumstances will any blame or legal responsibility be held against the publisher, or author, for any damages, reparation, or monetary loss due to the information contained within this book, either directly or indirectly.

Legal Notice:

This book is copyright protected. It is only for personal use. You cannot amend, distribute, sell, use, quote, or paraphrase any part, or the content within this book, without the consent of the author or publisher.

Disclaimer Notice:

Please note the information contained within this document is for educational and entertainment purposes only. All effort has been executed to present accurate, up-to-date, reliable, and complete information. No warranties of any kind are declared or implied. Readers acknowledge that the author is not engaging in the rendering of legal, financial, medical, or professional advice. The content within this book has been derived from various sources. Please consult a licensed professional before attempting any techniques outlined in this book.

By reading this document, the reader agrees that under no circumstances is the author responsible for any losses, direct or indirect, that are incurred as a result of the use of the information contained within this document, including, but not limited to, errors, omissions, or inaccuracies.

Free limited time bonus

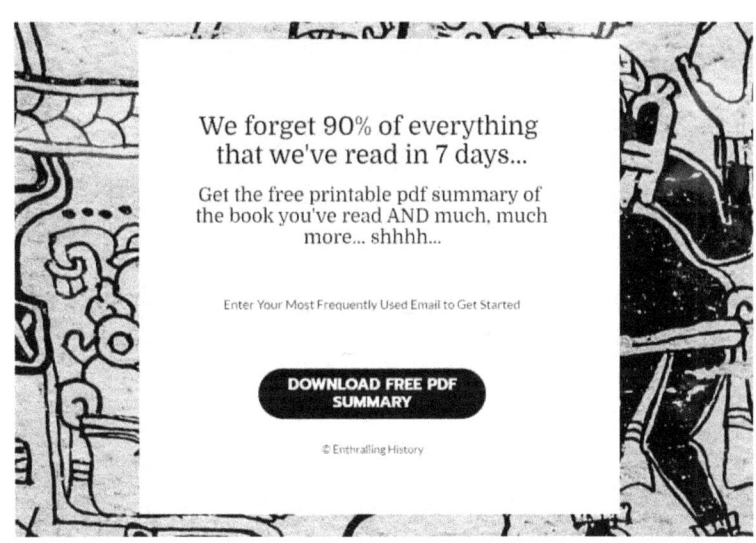

Stop for a moment. We have a free bonus set up for you. The problem is this: we forget 90% of everything that we read after 7 days. Crazy fact, right? Here's the solution: we've created a printable, 1-page pdf summary for this book that you're reading now. All you have to do to get your free pdf summary is to go to the following website: https://livetolearn.lpages.co/enthrallinghistory/

Or, Scan the QR code!

Once you do, it will be intuitive. Enjoy, and thank you!

Table of Contents

INTRODUCTION 1
CHAPTER 1: THE ORIGINS OF THE SLAVE TRADE 3
CHAPTER 2: THE ATLANTIC TRIANGULAR TRADE: A NETWORK OF EXPLOITATION 10
CHAPTER 3: THE HORRORS OF THE MIDDLE PASSAGE 23
CHAPTER 4: AFRICAN ROOTS: SOCIETIES UPROOTED BY THE SLAVE TRADE 30
CHAPTER 5: THE BUSINESS OF HUMAN TRAFFICKING 40
CHAPTER 6: PLANTATION SYSTEM IN THE NEW WORLD 49
CHAPTER 7: THE HUMAN TOLL OF THE SLAVE TRADE 58
CHAPTER 8: ABOLITION MOVEMENTS: THE FIGHT FOR FREEDOM AND EQUALITY 65
CHAPTER 9: THE LEGACY OF THE ATLANTIC SLAVE TRADE ... 78
CHAPTER 10: REEXAMINING HISTORY: CRITICAL PERSPECTIVES ON THE SLAVE TRADE 86
CONCLUSION 90
HERE'S ANOTHER BOOK BY ENTHRALLING HISTORY THAT YOU MIGHT LIKE 93
FREE LIMITED TIME BONUS 94
BIBLIOGRAPHY 95

Introduction

Elmina is a beautiful fishing town on Ghana's coast. It is the postcard type of spot that vacationers love to visit for its ocean breezes and charm. Towering above the harbor is Elmina Castle, located on a narrow promontory close to the Atlantic Ocean. However, it is not the fairytale castle of a Disney movie, and it was not the scene of happy endings. Elmina Castle is the oldest European building found in sub-Saharan Africa. It was a trading post, and the products contained within its walls were human beings. Elmina Castle was an integral part of the Atlantic slave trade, and its sinister history is part of an even darker tale.

The Atlantic slave trade remains one of the most devastating and controversial episodes in human history. Originating in the 15th century with the maritime exploration of European powers, the slave trade became a complex, transcontinental web that involved multiple nations and cultures and millions of human lives.

Over a period of roughly four centuries, it is estimated that more than twelve million Africans were forced from their homeland and subjected to the horrors of the Middle Passage—a gruesome voyage across the Atlantic—before being sold into slavery in the Americas.

The Atlantic slave trade did not begin in a vacuum. Slavery existed in Africa before the advent of European traders, albeit in a different form and scale. Europeans initially reached African shores in search of gold, spices, and other exotic goods. However, the discovery of the New World created an enormous demand for labor to exploit the natural resources of the Americas. Indigenous populations in the colonies suffered massive casualties from disease and overwork, necessitating an alternative labor force. Thus was born the transatlantic slave trade, a triangular system involving Europe, Africa, and the Americas.

The typical "triangle trade" began with European ships loaded with goods like firearms, alcohol, and textiles sailing to African coasts. These goods were exchanged for enslaved Africans, who were then shipped across the Atlantic. Upon their arrival in the Americas, the survivors of the Middle Passage were sold, and the ships were loaded with American goods like sugar, tobacco, and cotton, which would return to Europe. This cycle, which was repeated over the centuries, involved multiple European powers, including the Portuguese, Spanish, Dutch, British, and French.

A nuanced understanding of the Atlantic slave trade necessitates acknowledging the involvement of African states and tribes. Kingdoms like Dahomey, Asante, and Oyo played pivotal roles in capturing and selling their countrymen or rival tribes to European traders. For these states, the slave trade was a source of power, wealth, and access to crucial goods like firearms. Nevertheless, the internal dynamics were far from simple, as even within these benefiting states, opinions and involvement in the slave trade varied significantly, creating a complex narrative of complicity and victimhood.

The economic underpinning of the Atlantic slave trade was formidable. In Africa, the drain of a large segment of the population led to economic stagnation and social disintegration. Communities were torn apart, local economies were ruined, and technological and social progress were hampered. The societal fractures created by the slave trade had long-lasting impacts, contributing to political instability and underdevelopment in many African nations.

The Atlantic slave trade was a devastating chapter in human history, the consequences of which continue to reverberate today. Let us first examine how it all started.

Chapter 1: The Origins of the Slave Trade

Slavery existed in West Africa long before the Europeans arrived there. A robust market for human beings existed for centuries in the region.

Forced labor, including slavery, has a long and painful history, and it continues to exist in various forms today. Despite the universal condemnation it receives and the moral and ethical questions it raises, the institution of slavery has been rationalized historically—and sometimes contemporarily—through perceived economic and social necessities.

One of the most commonly cited reasons for forced labor and slavery has been the economic advantage of having a cheap or free labor force. Whether it was agricultural work in the American South, mining in colonial Africa, or modern-day sweatshops, the rationale often given is that low-cost labor provides economic growth and prosperity. Slavery provides a free labor force that enables business owners to maximize profits.

One of the darker aspects of the social justification for slavery was the idea that it provided a form of social control. It was thought that by subjugating a group of people, social hierarchies could be maintained more easily. The notion that certain groups were naturally suited for subjugation was used to legitimize forced labor. Though widely discredited and morally indefensible, this argument provided a convenient justification for those benefitting from the institution, especially during the time of the Atlantic slave trade.[1]

Muslim Slave Trade

There was a demand for forced human labor in North African markets, and rulers in West Africa were willing to fill the need. It is estimated that as many as nine million people were herded north along the trans-Saharan slave trade routes.[2]

One of the primary reasons Muslims engaged in the slave trade was the need for labor. Slaves were often used in agricultural settings, in mines, and as household servants. A labor-intensive economy created a demand for slaves.

Slave trading was a profitable enterprise and became an essential part of the economy for some Muslim states and traders. Slaves were considered valuable commodities and were traded along with goods like spices, textiles, and gold.

Ghanian historian Akosua Perbi has noted that indigenous slavery in Ghana and other parts of West Africa had been in existence since the 1st century CE. Forced labor came in various forms, such as indentured servitude, and in those areas that were not Muslim, slavery played a smaller role in the economy. However, these early markets were nowhere near as extensive as they became in later centuries.

---

[1] LDHI. (2023, September 8). *Slavery before the Trans-Atlantic Trade.* Retrieved from Africn Passages, Lowcountry Adaptations:
https://ldhi.library.cofc.edu/exhibits/show/africanpassageslowcountryadapt/introductionatlanticworld/slaverybeforetrade.

[2] Thothios.com. (2023, September 8). *The Causes and Effects of the Trans-Saharan Trade.* Retrieved from Thothios.com: https://www.thothios.com/c-1200-to-c-1450/unit-2-networks-of-exchange/trans-saharan-trade/.

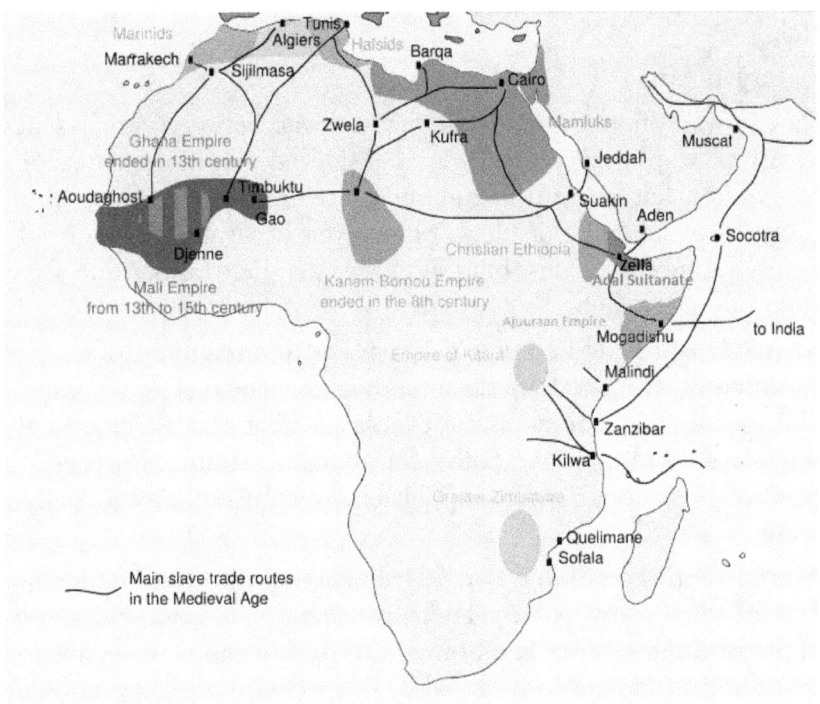

The major slave trade routes in Africa during the Middle Ages.
Runehelmet derived from Aliesin, CC BY-SA 3.0 <https://creativecommons.org/licenses/by-sa/3.0>, via Wikimedia Commons; https://commons.wikimedia.org/wiki/File:African_slave_trade.png

The trans-Sahara had slave trade routes to the Ghana Empire and the Mali Empire during the Middle Ages.

The Ghana Empire

The Ghana Empire was not located in what is now the modern state of Ghana. In fact, it was closer to Senegal. The Ghana Empire traded along the trans-Saharan routes, and slaves were part of its commercial transactions. The Ghana Empire was gone by the time of the Europeans' arrival in West Africa, but it did help lay the foundation of slave acquisition and sale in the region.

The Mali Empire

The Mali Empire was a major West African state in the Late Middle Ages. Ibn Battuta wrote about the wealth and prestige of Mansa Musa, who ruled Mali in the early 14th century. Slavery and human trafficking were part of the fabric of the Mali Empire. Mansa Musa reportedly owned thousands of slaves. Many of them worked in the copper mines of Mali.

Slavery in Africa

Slavery was often the consequence of war between small states in West Africa. Captured soldiers were considered part of the spoils of war. Africans often felt no remorse about enslaving their rivals because the latter were considered outsiders. Slaves were typically prisoners of war who were captured in raids, but there were people who became slaves to pay off outstanding debts.[3]

Islamic law provided some guidelines for the treatment of slaves that were different from other slave-holding societies. The Qur'an and Hadith (sayings and actions of the Prophet Muhammad) advise kindness toward slaves and provide paths for their freedom. However, these protections were often more applicable to Muslim slaves than non-Muslims.

Non-Muslim slaves often had fewer rights and protections compared to their Muslim counterparts. Their treatment varied depending on the time, place, and their masters. Some non-Muslim slaves were able to rise to significant positions of power, while others endured harsh conditions. Slaves who converted to Islam often received better treatment and had a greater chance of manumission.

While Islamic law offered some protections for slaves, these were not universally applied, and non-Muslim slaves often found themselves in precarious situations. The practice of castration, although not universally condoned, was a part of the slave trade and raises ethical and moral questions that continue to be subject to scholarly debate.

Castration was particularly practiced on slaves brought from Central and East Africa. Castrated males, often referred to as eunuchs, served in various capacities, including as guards for harems and high-ranking officials. Islamic law prohibits mutilation, but castration often took place before the slaves entered Islamic territories. It was typically done by non-Muslim traders. Castration was a risky procedure with a high mortality rate, making eunuchs highly valuable commodities.

An important difference between the trans-Saharan slave trade and the Atlantic slave trade is that in the former, slaves had certain rights that were to be respected. Some slaves (not all) could get married and own

---

[3] Pbs.org. (2023, September 8). *Confronting the Legacy of the African Slave Trade*. Retrieved from The Slave Kingdoms: http://www.pbs.org/wonders/Episodes/Epi3/slave_2.htm.

property, and there were instances where slaves were soldiers or held political power.

There were West African kingdoms that played a notable role as middlemen, capturing, trading, and selling slaves to Europeans and Muslims. These are referred to as the "Slave Kingdoms," and they had various motivations for participating in the slave trade. They had a well-developed system in place by the time the Europeans arrived.

The dynamics of power perhaps stimulated the slave trade the most. The subjugation of rival groups and the assertion of social hierarchies were aided through participation in the slave trade. In other words, a kingdom could get rid of its enemies and potential rebels by selling them.

African kingdoms also wanted European goods, especially firearms. In fact, it could be argued that the arms trade was almost symbiotic with the slave trade. A vicious cycle was created where an African kingdom, armed with European weapons, could capture even more slaves to be sold for other products.

In a sense, the slave trade became highly addictive. Revenues generated from selling war captives allowed kingdoms to have resources that were otherwise not available. In some instances, slavery was an economic pillar that supported everything, including public infrastructure.

Economic gains strengthened the military, and internal power consolidations were notable among the kingdoms on the Atlantic coast of Africa. There is no question that those states benefited from the trade, but they ultimately created a system that had devastating impacts on Africa.

The Kingdom of Dahomey

Located in what is now Benin, the Kingdom of Dahomey's economy was heavily reliant on the slave trade, and the kingdom viewed it as an avenue for economic growth and political dominance.

Dahomey was an absolute monarchy with a stratified society. The kingdom was militaristic, and taking captives to be sold as slaves was a political objective. Slavery brought in revenue that financed military and political ventures. European firearms that were received in exchange for slaves expanded Dahomey's military capabilities.[4]

Dahomey was a major supplier during the Atlantic slave trade. Even though some pressure was placed on the kingdom to reduce its participation in the sale of humans, it is estimated that Dahomey contributed as much as 20 percent to the total slave trade in the late 18th century.[5]

The Asante Empire

Another major player in the slave trade was Asante. Located in what is now Ghana, the Asante Empire (also known as the Ashanti Empire) traded gold, ivory, and slaves in exchange for European goods. The Asante used the slave trade as a means of consolidating power over neighboring states and reinforcing social hierarchies. The Asante Empire had an elaborate political structure that was funded by slave commerce.

Slaves were used in households, on farms, or in the military. The Asante viewed slavery as a natural institution that was time-honored. It had been practiced by their ancestors and had the sanction and approval of the gods.[6]

The Oyo Empire

The Oyo Empire was a powerful Yoruba state located in what is now Nigeria. The slave trade allowed the Oyo to sustain a complex military and political system. As firearms became increasingly essential for any military advantage, the Oyo Empire discovered it was beneficial to trade slaves for European weapons.

The Oyo acquired access to the Atlantic coast through subordinate kingdoms, thus enabling the empire to have access to European trade. The Oyo Empire used slave labor on royal farms, and any surplus labor was sold. Ultimately, its dependence on the slave trade as a source of revenue caused serious problems as the Atlantic slave trade began to subside.[7]

---

[4] McKenna, A. (2023, September 8). *Dahomey*. Retrieved from Britannica.com: https://www.britannica.com/place/Dahomey-historical-kingdom-Africa.

[5] Team, T. E. (2019, November 11). *The History of the Kingdom of Dahomey*. Retrieved from Blackhistorymonth.org: https://www.blackhistorymonth.org.uk/article/section/pre-colonial-history/the-history-of-the-kingdom-of-dahomey/.

[6] Matthews, L. (2020, September 23). *Slavery in the Asante Empire of West Africa*.

[7] Slaveryandremembrance.org. (2023, September 8). *Oyo Empire*. Retrieved from Slaveryandremembrance.org:
https://slaveryandremembrance.org/articles/article/?id=A0121#:~:text=Enslaved%20laborers%20

The Kingdom of Kongo

The Kingdom of Kongo was in modern-day Angola and the Democratic Republic of Congo. It was the dominant state of the West-Central African coast. Kongo provided the largest number of slaves who were shipped to the Americas. This has been verified by genetic studies that show a legacy of Kongolese people in American and Caribbean genomes.

The Kongolese traded primarily with the Portuguese, and the slave trade quickly became a lucrative business. The Kongo Civil Wars (1665-1709) provided an enormous supply of war captives, who, in turn, were sold to the Portuguese and other local slavers.

Interestingly, the rulers of Kongo became concerned with the extent of slavery in their territory. The letters of Afonso I, King of Kongo, who ruled from 1509 to 1543, show the anger he had for the increasing Portuguese demand for slaves. The trouble was that by the time the king expressed his concern, the slave trade was already becoming ingrained in Kongo. There was not much he could do to stop it.

The dominance of the slave trade did not stop local people from resisting. The Antonian rebellion of the 18th century had thousands of followers; opposition to the slave trade was one of the triggers of the revolt. However, the rebellion ultimately failed.[8]

In Summary

The arrival of the Europeans in the 14th century stimulated the slave trade to levels that were not seen before. Europeans had a pressing need for forced labor, and the Europeans had what the African rulers wanted and needed: guns and gunpowder.

A devil's bargain was in the making. The result was a partnership that, over the years, would serve to deplete Africa of manpower and create governments that depended on raiding and warfare to thrive.

---

provided%20food%20for,and%20eventually%20ended%2C%20Oyo%20suffered.
[8] Pasciuto, G. (2022, December 21). *7 Facts About the Kingdom of Kongo: Africa's Great Catholic State*. Retrieved from Thecollector.com: https://www.thecollector.com/kingdom-of-kongo-great-catholic-state/.

Chapter 2: The Atlantic Triangular Trade: A Network of Exploitation

The Atlantic slave trade was not just a single trade route going from one port of call to another. A triangular trade network arose that involved nation-states in Europe, Africa, and North and South America. Goods went from Europe to Africa, enslaved people were then shipped to the Americas, and commodities like tobacco went to Europe, with the process beginning all over again. Each nation had its own reasons to engage in the slave trade, and all of them profited in some way, although, of course, some nations were more negatively impacted than others.

There were five major European participants in the slave trade: Portugal, Spain, the Netherlands, France, and Great Britain. Some had moral restrictions, while others were out for pure profit. Each had a modus operandi that enabled them to manage competition while getting the forced labor they required.

The Age of Portuguese Exploration

Henry the Navigator was a pious man by all accounts. He was a patron of religious orders and had a desire to spread Christianity to other parts of the world. Prince Henry was also interested in navigation and sailing.

Prince Henry was the son of King John I and Queen Philippa of Portugal. He was born in 1394 in Portugal. He was not a patron of the arts, as was common among the aristocracy then. Instead, he became a patron of the seas. Henry was interested in technological advances that could help his country. He sparked the Age of Exploration in Portugal, which would eventually lead to a commercial empire that was beyond imagination when he was born.

Henry was the sponsor of numerous expeditions, opening the door to long-distance voyages. Henry's patronage of maritime inventions resulted in technological improvements, such as cartography, better use of the astrolabe, and the quadrant. Improvements were also made in ship design, allowing Portuguese caravels to go out into the deep sea.

Henry was interested in exploration but not for the sake of finding new things and new people. Henry's primary objective was to discover a sea route to Asia that would allow Portugal to have access to spices and other luxury markets. He wanted to bypass the Muslim monopoly of trade routes to the Far East.

This deeply religious man no doubt had little idea that one of the byproducts of his interest in navigation was the creation of a monstrous commercial enterprise. At the beginning of the 14th century, Portugal was a relatively poor country. It was not much more than a rocky slice of land along the Atlantic coast with very little prospects of wealth. That was going to change dramatically. And the reason why was that Portugal turned its attention westward.

The Atlantic Ocean south of Gibraltar was a great unknown, and the Portuguese began sailing into those waters as the 15th century progressed. The country benefited from other European nations being in constant war with each other. Voyage improvements were made, and Portuguese commerce improved.

A defining moment came with the Treaty of Alcáçovas in 1479. Portugal agreed to surrender any claim to the Canary Islands in exchange for the rights to any lands conquered outside of Europe. A line was drawn through the Canary Islands, and everything south of the line and south of the Canary Islands would be Portugal's if the Portuguese successfully conquered it.

Portuguese ships sailed down the west coast of Africa, visiting lands Europe had never explored before. An expedition led by Bartolomeu Dias in 1485 rounded the southern tip of Africa before a mutiny forced the expedition to go home.

Other European countries became interested in overseas exploration, particularly Spain. Spain and Portugal agreed to a treaty brokered by the pope to avoid possible war. The Treaty of Tordesillas in 1494 created a line of demarcation that expanded on the earlier boundaries created by Alcáçovas. The new terms specified a new line running north and south. Portugal would have a claim to all lands south of the Canary Islands, provided they were east of the new line. Those lands included West Africa.[9]

Portuguese expeditions permitted Europeans to become more familiar with West Africa. Gradually, a network of forts and trading posts was created along the coast to facilitate commerce. These would be places where ships could take on supplies and where commercial opportunities could be exploited. Early settlements included Arguin Island (1445) and São Jorge da Mina (Elmina Castle, 1482). São Tomé was founded in 1493. More outposts would be created as Portugal gradually moved farther south down the coast.

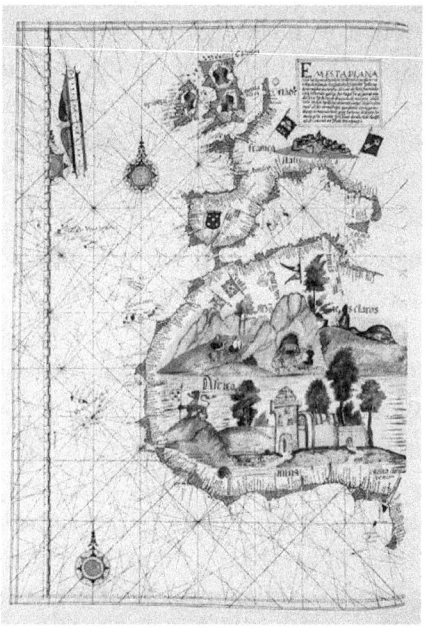

A Portuguese map from the 16ᵗʰ century. The large castle in West Africa symbolizes Elmina Castle.
https://commons.wikimedia.org/wiki/File:L%C3%A1zaro_Luis_1563.jpg

---

[9] Williams, F. G. (2023, September 14). *The Rise and Fall of Portugal's Maritime Empire, a Cautionary Tale?* Retrieved from Byustudies.byu.edu: https://byustudies.byu.edu/article/the-rise-and-fall-of-portugals-maritime-empire-a-cautionary-tale/.

The Allure of Slavery

Madeira, Cape Verde, and São Tomé became centers of sugar cultivation as plantations sprang up to supply growing European demand. These plantations required large amounts of labor, and forced labor was an answer to the labor shortage.

Early contacts with African kingdoms on the West African coast involved the purchase of gold, but the need for enslaved people to work on the plantations caused the Portuguese to begin trading in humans.

Portugal did not have any interest in going deep into Africa since that would mean it would have to manage large amounts of territory inland and on the coast. It made more sense to have trading posts on the coastline and allow the Africans to bring slaves to them.

The Portuguese had one product that created great interest among African rulers. Firearms were not very prevalent in Africa at that time, and the Portuguese were ready suppliers. The monarchs of the Oyo Empire, the Asante Empire, and the Kingdom of Kongo had an opportunity to get a hold of military technology that could enable them to expand their territories and subjugate other people. A symbiotic relationship developed between the Portuguese and the African kingdoms.

A close relationship between Portugal and the Kingdom of Kongo emerged in the late 15th century. The Portuguese extended their dominance in Kongo through treaties, trade alliances, and military exploits that capitalized on internal conflicts within Kongo and the neighboring Kingdom of Ndongo.

Portugal would start to transport slaves to Brazil in the 16th century, and the volume of traffic expanded as that Portuguese colony prospered.

An interesting dichotomy developed in Spain and Portugal as it related to slavery. Both countries were devoutly Catholic, and it was their policy to try to convert as many people to Catholicism as possible. In spite of the missionary zeal, however, both countries appeared to have no problem with the concept of slavery. It did not seem to matter that Spain and Portugal were buying and selling people who converted to Catholicism. It was all a matter of business; any religious ties between the enslaved and the slaver were coincidental.

Spain and the New World

The Spanish viewed the Americas as a place to win converts to the Catholic faith, which would counterbalance gains made by Protestants in Europe. Still, the Spanish primarily viewed the New World as a place to make a considerable profit. The economic opportunities only grew more significant with the conquest of Mexico and Peru.

The Spanish developed unique ways of incorporating forced labor into the colonial economy. An interesting means by which the Spanish forced the indigenous population to toil for them was through the encomienda system.

The encomienda system permitted settlers (*encomenderos*) to obtain a grant from the Spanish Crown that gave them control over indigenous communities. The *encomenderos* were required to provide protection and Christian education to those indigenous people placed under their charge. The natives, in return, would offer tribute in the form of labor. It looked on paper as a form of feudalism. However, it developed into something entirely different.

The encomienda system eventually developed into a labor system that was unequal and coercive. Indigenous people were subjected to harsh working conditions, often being forced to work in mines or on plantations for long hours without adequate compensation or rights. The Spanish settlers held enormous power over the labor force, which led to mistreatment and exploitation.

The Valladolid Debate

The abuse of indigenous people did not go unnoticed. Bartolomé de las Casas was a Dominican friar living in the Spanish New World. He started out as an *encomendero* but underwent a moral transformation and entered the clergy. He was horrified at the behavior of his fellow countrymen and refused to be silent. His concerns and those expressed by others prompted the Spanish Crown to organize a series of discussions in 1550 on how indigenous people in the Americas were being treated. These were known as the Valladolid debate.

Discussions took place on August 15th, 1550, in Valladolid, Spain, and there was a vigorous argument about the pros and cons of how indigenous people were being abused. Juan Ginés de Sepúlveda was a humanist scholar who defended Spanish colonization. He believed that the subjugation of the natives was appropriate.

De Sepúlveda argued primitive people had no understanding of reason and morality. Spain, de Sepúlveda reasoned, was morally obligated to conquer and civilize native people. He also maintained that the indigenous people were natural slaves. They were suited to slavery, and their perceived inferiority justified their subjugation by the Spanish. His final argument was that these people would be better off under Spanish rule than they had been before.

Las Casas was up for making his case. He countered that indigenous people had their own cultures and ways of life that deserved as much respect as those of Europeans. He stated they were human and deserving of respect and dignity. He contended that the Spanish conquest only brought misery. His final point stressed that indigenous people should be allowed to live according to their own traditions and beliefs. The judges ultimately ruled in favor of the las Casas.

The decision that came out from this debate was that the native people were human and deserving of the same rights and protections as Europeans. Las Casas would continue to advocate for fundamental human rights and, in 1552, published the book *A Short Account of the Destruction of the Indies*, which details the abuse of indigenous people caused by the encomienda system.[10]

The result of the Valladolid debate was an ordinance issued by Philip II in 1573 that redefined future Spanish discoveries. The Spanish king declared that those discoveries would not be labeled as conquests but instead as pacifications. It was a significant step forward in the treatment of indigenous people.

However, there was no step forward on the question of slavery. There is no evidence that life improved for the vast majority of natives in the Spanish colonies.[11]

The Asiento System

A new chapter in the labor relations of the Americas happened in the late 16th century. The Spanish Crown introduced the asiento system, a contractual arrangement between Spain and various European entities,

---

[10] History Skills. (2023, September 14). *The Valladolid Debate: When Europeans Argued About Whether Indigenous People Were Human*. Retrieved from Historyskills.com: https://www.historyskills.com/classroom/year-8/valladolid-debate/.
[11] Lyons, M. (2023, August). *The Valladolid Debate on the Rights of Indigenous People*. Retrieved from History Today: https://www.historytoday.com/archive/months-past/valladolid-debate-rights-indigenous-people.

which included merchants and companies. Those who held the contracts, known as *asientistas*, were given the exclusive right to supply African slaves to the Spanish colonies within a determined period of time. The Spanish Crown would receive taxes and fees for this privilege. This arrangement effectively bypassed the question of enslaving Native Americans.

The asiento system provided a legal framework and incentive for the mass trafficking of Africans, thus institutionalizing a supply chain of slaves to the Spanish New World. It represented a calculated market approach to human-forced labor. Humans were reduced to labor units to be bought and sold. Profits would be maximized by acquiring slaves at the lowest possible cost and selling them to the highest bidder. It would be pure exploitation devoid of any human rights.

Estimates suggest that approximately 1.3 million African slaves were sent to Spanish territories in the New World. They would be used in labor-intensive enterprises, such as sugarcane plantations in Cuba.

The asiento system played a role in the social hierarchy of Spanish-held America. Although the indigenous population was marginalized, they did have some rights in Spanish America. Enslaved Africans had none and, consequently, were permanently fixed at the bottom of the social structure.

The Dutch Participation in the Slave Trade

The Dutch did not play a significant role in the early days of the Atlantic slave trade because the Netherlands was vigorously fighting for its independence from Spain. However, their role began to expand in the 17th century when the Dutch West India Company was founded in 1621.

There is a chilling feature to that commercial enterprise. The Dutch West India Company was not interested in saving souls. It was concerned with business, and slave dealing was part of that business. The Dutch West India Company's sphere of influence included areas that bordered the Atlantic Ocean, such as West Africa and the Americas. What the Dutch West India Company considered the West Indies included Brazil, Berbice, Guyana, Essequibo, Surinam, and the Antilles.

The First Dutch West India Company lasted from 1621 to 1674, when it was dissolved. The Second Dutch West India Company was formed in 1674 and was primarily concerned with the slave trade. It had a monopoly on the Dutch slave trade until 1734.[12]

The Dutch West India Company focused on securing a commanding position in the Atlantic slave trade. Although its members were primarily merchants, the company had no problem conducting military affairs. The Portuguese possession of Elmina was seized in 1637, which was followed by the capture of Luanda in 1641.

The Dutch increased their presence in the Atlantic slave trade by either seizing existing forts on the African Atlantic coast or establishing them. In addition to Elmina, the Dutch West India Company's presence in West Africa included:
- Fort Nassau
- Fort Amsterdam
- Fort Vredenburgh
- Fort Lijdzaamheid
- Fort Crèvecœur
- Fort Dixcove
- Fort Batenstein
- Fort San Sebastian
- Fort St. Anthony at Axim

All of these forts were located on the coast of what is now present-day Ghana. The Dutch had commercial entrepots from present-day Ghana all the way down the coast to Namibia.

Managing colonies was expensive, and instead of carving out provinces to colonize, the company concentrated on supplying English, French, and Spanish colonies with forced labor. The Dutch West India Company was the largest slave trading company of its time. Between 1658 and 1674, it traded approximately 53,600 Africans. Modern estimates show that the Dutch were responsible for the forced migration of anywhere from 500,000 to 600,000 enslaved Africans to the New World.[13]

The French and Sugar

Guadeloupe and Martinique are specks of land floating in the Caribbean. Today, they are tourist destinations noted for their natural

---

[12] Zeeuwsarchief.ni. (2023, September 14). *The Voyage-History*. Retrieved from Zeeuwsarchief.ni: https://www.zeeuwsarchief.nl/en/themepage/slave-voyage-aboard-the-unity/the-voyage-history/.

[13] Thiebaut, R. (2023, April 26). *The WIC, The Dutch West India Company*. Retrieved from Projectmanifest.eu: https://www.projectmanifest.eu/the-wic-the-dutch-west-india-company-en-fr/.

beauty and snorkeling. Three hundred years ago, however, these islands were the sources of immense wealth for France. Indeed, the profit derived from these plots of land was substantially more than all the British colonies in North America could produce.

Europe had a sweet tooth, and the sugar craving was a Continental addiction. The islands in the Caribbean were ideal for the cultivation and production of sugar. The process was labor intensive, and forced labor was the cheapest means of getting the job done.

France became involved in the slave trade in the 16th century and was one of the key European powers involved in the Atlantic slave trade due to the immense profits that could be made.

Martinique and Guadeloupe were not the only destinations for French slave ships, though. The most lucrative French colony in the Caribbean was Saint-Domingue, now known as Haiti. Although sugar was the primary commodity, coffee, indigo, and cotton were also produced in this colony.

Historians estimate that more than one million slaves were exported from West Africa to French Caribbean territories. Of these, Saint-Domingue was the primary port of call. Nearly 800,000 enslaved people were shipped there.[14]

Posts in West Africa

The French established trading posts and forts in West Africa to expedite shipping. Several were prominent ports in the Atlantic slave trade.

- Ouidah, located in Benin, was a significant slave trading post under the French flag. Ouidah was the primary hub from which slaves were transported to the French colonies.
- Goree Island traded hands frequently and was under British and Dutch control at one time or another. Goree Island is located off the coast of Senegal. It was a gathering place for newly acquired slaves that would be sent to the Americas.
- Saint-Louis was situated at the mouth of the Senegal River. Although Saint-Louis originally was a trading post for gum arabic and other commodities, it eventually became heavily involved in the slave trade.

---

[14] Slavery and Remembrance. (2023, September 14). *French Slave Trade*. Retrieved from Slaveryandremembrance.org: https://slaveryandremembrance.org/articles/article/?id=A0097.

- Juda Point was a significant slave trading post in the Bight of Benin. Juda Point frequently changed hands.

Warfare was not the only reason why a trading post would fly different flags. Treaties and other geopolitical factors were involved. Moreover, local African rulers might be in an alliance and then later in conflict with the French (or another European nation), complicating matters.

The irony of France's participation in the slave trade is that this country was at the forefront of spreading ideals of liberty and human rights during the Enlightenment. France would abolish slavery in 1794, but this didn't last long. Napoleon Bonaparte reestablished it in 1802. Saint-Domingue would continue to be a destination for slave cargo right up until the success of the Haitian Revolution.

Great Britain and Human Cargo

Great Britain was first involved in the slave trade in the 16th century and became the world's leading slave-trading power by the end of the 18th century. British possessions in the Caribbean, such as Jamaica, Barbados, and Antigua, were common destinations for enslaved people, but those were not the only places where slave ships went. Slave labor was also used in tobacco, cotton, and indigo plantations in the American colonies, particularly in Virginia and the Carolinas. The British also took advantage of the Spanish asiento system and furnished the Spanish possessions with forced labor.

The slave trade became an integral part of the British economy. Liverpool, Bristol, and London became important hubs for the traffic in human beings.

Profits poured into Great Britain from the plantations, making merchants rich and eventually financing the early stages of the Industrial Revolution. Many aspiring people in business became extremely wealthy thanks to the sweat and toil of enslaved Africans.

The Power of Credit

The slave trade was profitable, but it did have risks. Slave ships could be on the high seas for months, and slave traders would not realize any profits until the final sales were made. Plantation owners would only realize the benefits of their purchases once their crops had been sold. Added to all of this was the possibility of slave ships being intercepted by pirates or sinking with all of their cargo. The British thrived in spite of all these dangers. Their secret? Credit.

The British financial system developed over the years, with the Bank of England being the central point. Bills of credit became the means of financing the slave trade and permitting all business parties to make it through substantial time lags. Insurance policies gradually reduced the risk of losing cargo on the high seas. Profit margins consequently increased as the risks went down.

Great Britain would eventually abolish slavery in 1834. By that time, immense fortunes had been made. The British system of business included investors, insurance companies, banking houses, and other people involved in the transport and sale of enslaved people. More than 3.2 million Africans were shipped to the Western Hemisphere by the British, helping the island nation to become the most influential European country of the time.[15]

The Points of the Triangles

As mentioned, triangles were formed, with products being shipped from one place to another until that ship finally arrived back at the original point on the triangle. Several transatlantic slave routes gradually developed. These had ports of origin and stops along the way, with the ultimate destination being somewhere in the Americas.

- European Ports

The principal triangle ports in Britain were Liverpool, Bristol, and London. The French ports were Nantes, Bordeaux, and La Rochelle. Ports from which slave ships would originally set sail in Portugal and Spain were Lisbon and Seville or Cádiz, respectively. The Dutch used Amsterdam.

- West African Ports of Call

The African destinations were the West and Central African coastlines. The Gold Coast (Ghana), the Slave Coast (Benin and Togo), the Windward Coast (modern-day Liberia and Côte d'Ivoire), the Bights of Benin and Biafra, and Angola were destinations for slave ships to purchase and load human cargo.

- The Americas

The final destinations in the Caribbean included Jamaica, Barbados, Cuba, and Saint-Domingue. North American ports included Charleston, South Carolina, and ports along the Virginia coast.

---

[15] Slavery and Remembrance. (2023, September 14). *British Slave Trade*. Retrieved from Slaveryandremembrance.org: https://slaveryandremembrance.org/articles/article/?id=A0116.

Brazil was the largest importer of African slaves in the Americas. Many ships docked at Salvador in the state of Bahia. Because enslaved people were also used in mining, Cartagena in present-day Colombia was a port of call.

A Typical Triangle Voyage

Because Great Britain was a dominant player in the Atlantic slave trade, we are going to describe the typical voyage of a British slave vessel.

The ship would be docked in Liverpool and take on trading goods and supplies. These could be textiles such as woolen cloth, cotton, guns, ammunition, alcohol like rum or brandy, and other manufactured items that would appeal to African consumers. Once fully stocked, the ship would leave the harbor, head out into the open water, and head toward Africa.

Merchants wanted to do business in areas that were amenable to Great Britain. Consequently, destinations could be the Gold Coast, the Bight of Benin, or the Bight of Biafra. The trading of goods for people would take place in a convenient place, and then the ship would embark on the second leg of the triangle.

Traveling to the Americas would hopefully not face any significant disturbances, but captains could expect a certain number of enslaved people to die on the way. There were several ports from which to choose. Kingston, Jamaica, was a major destination. The ship might also head to Charleston, South Carolina, where enslaved people would be sold to toil on tobacco or cotton plantations. Once the Africans disembarked, they would be fed more and prepared for the auction block.

The last leg of the trip would be back to the home port, which in this case was Liverpool. What was once occupied by chained people was piled high with products like sugar, rum, tobacco, and cotton. These products would be sold to domestic consumers or manufacturers who would produce products to be sold on the next voyage.

The Profit Margin

The slave trade was certainly not pro bono work. Investors expected profits, which would depend on multiple factors. Merchants would have to deduct the cost of outfitting and crewing the ships and the goods that were traded. If the demand was not as high, not as many enslaved people would be purchased. There was also the casualty rate on the high sea. Every time an enslaved person died, it meant there was that less money to be realized. The possibility of the ship being lost in a storm or attacked by pirates was a possibility, although these losses could be covered by insurance. The best that historians can estimate from sources, such as letters, ship logs, and financial records, is that the profit margin from a slave triangle voyage could be as low as 5 percent or as high as 20 percent per voyage.

In Summary

Slavery was a profitable enterprise, and many merchants got rich dealing in humans. Many European nations, including Denmark and Sweden, were involved in the Atlantic slave trade during its heyday. The asiento system was a business opportunity that was exploited by many involved in the Atlantic slave trade as the years rolled by. Commerce was heavily influenced by the slave trade, and maritime trade routes were gradually established. These would substantially affect the development of the economies of the New World and Europe.

Chapter 3: The Horrors of the Middle Passage

The Atlantic slave trade evolved so that by the 17th century, it was a well-established process whereby enslaved people were transported from Africa to the Western and Southern Hemispheres. Millions of Africans were placed in the holds of slave ships, some of which were specifically designed for human cargo. The route would be called the Middle Passage, and it was the highway to hell for many people.

The voyage typically lasted eighty days but could be longer due to the weather. The ships that were used were usually small schooners or purpose-built slave ships. Crews packed humans closely together on or below decks with little space to sit up or move around. Ventilation was minimal, and water was scarce.

The Ships

The idea behind shipping humans across the Atlantic was rather simple yet horrendous. The more people one could pack into the holds of the ship, the better the chances were of one making a profit. Ship captains had to accept that perhaps 15 percent or more of Africans would die before reaching the slave markets.

A small sloop might carry up to twenty enslaved people, while a three-masted vessel might have as many as nine hundred individuals. In the 1750s, Liverpool was a leading port for slave commerce. There, ships were built specifically for the slave trade.

The Liverpool ship model had some distinct features. The vessel had a lower deck beneath the main deck where hundreds of enslaved people could be detained for the passage. Air holes carved out of the hull above the water line allowed the living cargo stuffed inside the ship to breathe.

There was always the possibility of an enslaved person trying to commit suicide. Netting was installed around the ship's rails to prevent anyone from taking a leap into the ocean. A wooden barrier was constructed at midship. The crew would be able to retreat to this barrier if an uprising occurred and shoot guns and small cannons into an insurgent crowd.

A slave ship was easy to identify on the open sea because no shipbuilder would cut holes into the side of the hull if commodities like sugar were being transported.[16] Another means of identifying a slave ship was the stench that came from the bowels of the boat. Urine, feces, vomit, and other human excretions would be carried on the breeze, so a port would know a slave ship was coming in before the vessel was even spotted.[17]

The Smell of Despair

Accounts exist from people who experienced the crossing of the Middle Passage. Their stories give a detailed description of what happened below the deck. Olaudah Equiano explained his experience in a book he published in 1789.

"The closeness of the place, and the heat of the climate, added to the number in the ship, which was so crowded that each had scarcely room to turn himself, almost suffocated us. This produced copious perspirations, so that the air soon became unfit for respiration, from a variety of loathsome smells, and brought on a sickness among the slaves, of which many died, thus falling victims to the improvident avarice, as I may call it, of their purchasers. This wretched situation was again aggravated by the galling of the chains, now become insupportable; and the filth of the necessary tubs, into which the children often fell, and were almost suffocated. The shrieks of the women, and the groans of the

---

[16] When transporting sugar back to the home port, these holes would be sealed or covered so water would not damage the product.

[17] Rediker, M. (2021, December 14). *The Transatlantic Slave Trade Ships: Trajectories of Death and Violence Across the Ocean*. Retrieved from Thefunambulist.net:
https://thefunambulist.net/magazine/the-ocean/the-transatlantic-slave-trade-ships-trajectories-of-death-and-violence-across-the-ocean.

dying, rendered the whole a scene of horror almost inconceivable."[18]

Corroboration is an essential part of historical research. It allows us to verify what one person says in relation to another person's comments about a historical event. Dr. Alexander Falconbridge, a surgeon on several slave ships, confirmed Equiano's narrative about the conditions below deck. His reminisces about his experiences were published in 1788.

"The hardships and inconveniences suffered by the Negroes during the passage are scarcely to be enumerated or conceived ... But the exclusion of fresh air is among the most intolerable ... the Negroes' rooms soon grow intolerable hot. The confined air, rendered noxious by the effluvia exhaled from their bodies and being repeatedly breathed, soon produces fevers and fluxes which generally carries off great numbers of them ...

"During the voyages I made, I was frequently witness to the fatal effects of this exclusion of fresh air ... The deck, that is the floor of their rooms, was so covered with the blood and mucus which had proceeded from them in consequence of the flux, that it resembled a slaughter-house. It is not in the power of the human imagination to picture a situation more dreadful or disgusting."[19]

The intensity of the stench was no doubt determined by how the living cargo was packed. Loose packing meant fewer enslaved people were in the hold of the ship with the hopes that a more significant percentage of enslaved people would arrive at port alive. Tight packing, on the other hand, meant more slaves would be crammed into the space below deck. The intent there was to absorb any casualties in the hopes that volume would generate greater profit.[20]

---

[18] Rediker, M. (2021, December 14). *The Transatlantic Slave Trade Ships: Trajectories of Death and Violence Across the Ocean*. Retrieved from Thefunambulist.net: https://thefunambulist.net/magazine/the-ocean/the-transatlantic-slave-trade-ships-trajectories-of-death-and-violence-across-the-ocean.

[19] National Park Service. (2023, September 17). *The Middle Passage*. Retrieved from Nps.gov: https://www.nps.gov/articles/the-middle-passage.htm.

[20] Slavery and Remembrance. (2023, September 17). *Middle Passage*. Retrieved from slaveryandremembrance.org: https://slaveryandremembrance.org/articles/article/?id=A0032.

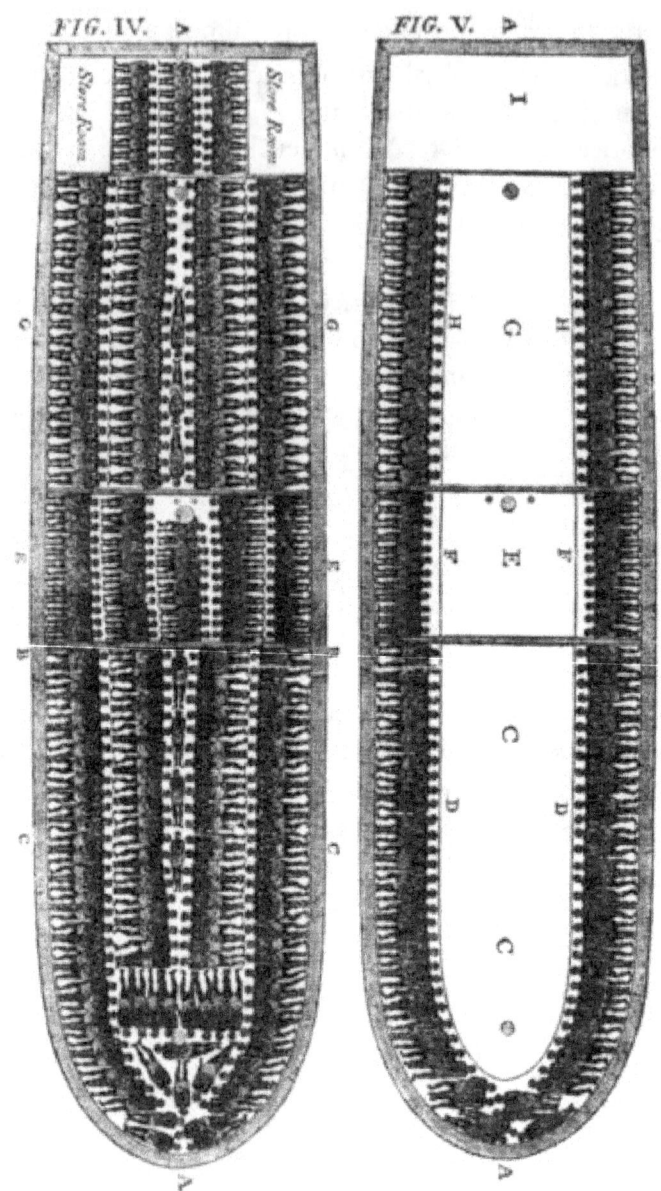

Diagram of a slave ship.
https://commons.wikimedia.org/wiki/File:Slave_ship_diagram.png

Families in Bondage

The chaos below deck was made worse by the different ethnicities chained to the boards. Because slave ships made several stops on the coast, having multiple national groups, each with a separate language, below deck was possible. The ship captain would deliberately mix different language groups to limit the chances of collective resistance or mutinies. This did not prohibit communication, however. Enslaved people would use signs, invent new words, and use percussion against the wooden ships to communicate with each other.

A sense of community would gradually form, with slaves referring to each other as "brother" or "sister" despite not being related to each other. Resistance was organized in subtle ways. When a few slaves refused to eat, others would take it as a sign to protest treatment. This practice was common. The slave ships carried an instrument called a speculum oris, which was used to pry open a person's mouth and allow food to be poured in.[21]

Slaves were fed twice a day, and if the weather permitted, they would be brought up on deck to get some exercise. The exercise time allowed the crew to go down and clean. Any dead bodies were thrown overboard, which explained why sharks and other predatory fish could often be found trailing a slave ship. When a vessel reached its final destination, the slaves were fed and cleaned to bring a higher price on the trading block. However, those who could not be sold were left for dead.[22]

Mortality rates were always a problem, and it was essential to get the enslaved Africans alive and well to port as soon as possible. Sometimes, there would be delays as the ships went up the African coast to purchase even more slaves. Robert Livingston, the third lord of Livingston Manor, reported to a fellow businessman on July 29th, 1749, the casualty lists of the slave ship *Rhode Island*:

"We have thank God had the good fortune of haveing one of our Guinea Sloops come in, tho after along passage of 79 days in which time they buryed 37 Slaves & Since 3 more & 2 more likely to die which is an accident not to be helped, and which if had not happened we Should have made a Golden Voyage but as it is there will not be much left I fear, unless the other Sloop meets with better Luck."[23]

---

[21] Rediker, M. (2021, December 14). *The Transatlantic Slave Trade Ships: Trajectories of Death and Violence Across the Ocean.*

[22] Ushistory.org. (2023, September 17). *The Middle Passage.* Retrieved from Ushistory.org: https://www.ushistory.org/us/6b.asp.

[23] The Gilder Lehrman Institute. (2023, September 17). *The Middle Passage, 1749.* Retrieved from Gilderlehman.org: https://www.gilderlehrman.org/history-resources/spotlight-primary-

The *Rhode Island* originally had 120 enslaved people on board, of which approximately one-third perished. Casualty figures that high meant the voyage was a financial loss.[24]

Slave Rebellions

There are over four hundred recorded instances of slave rebellions on the slave ships. Dr. Alexander Falconbridge gives us an explanation of why the slaves would rise up:

"As very few of the Negroes can so far brook [tolerate] the loss of their liberty and the hardships they endure, they are ever on the watch to take advantage of the least negligence in their oppressors. Insurrections are frequently the consequence, which are seldom expressed without much bloodshed. Sometimes, they are successful, and the whole ship's company is cut off."[25]

Approximately one in ten slave ships experienced resistance from enslaved Africans. Senegambia (a region that today incorporates Senegal, The Gambia, and Guinea-Bissau) had the highest incidence of rebellion on slave ships of any area in Africa. The resistance might be acts of defiance, such as a hunger strike, attempts to jump overboard, or a full-on battle with the sailors. Rebellions could result in a ship being sunk due to fire or a major explosion. Crews were outnumbered, but they had firearms, which they used to fight back and quell the revolt.[26]

There were several prominent slave maritime uprisings:

- The *Leusden* (1738)

The *Leusden* was carrying over seven hundred enslaved people when it was caught in a storm. The ship capsized, and the sailors were able to escape. Before they did, they nailed the hatches to the deck to prevent a slave uprising, which led to the loss of hundreds of lives. The *Leusden* disaster was one of the greatest losses of life during the days of the Middle Passage.

---

source/middle-passage-1749.

[24] The Gilder Lehrman Institute. (2023, September 17). *The Middle Passage, 1749.*

[25] PBS.org. (2023, September 17). *Insurrection on Board a Slave Ship.* Retrieved from Pbs.org: https://www.pbs.org/wgbh/aia/part1/1h317.html.

[26] Slavery and Remembrance. (2023, September 17). *Slave Ship Mutinies.* Retrieved from Slaveryandremembrance.org: https://slaveryandremembrance.org/articles/article/?id=A0035.

- The *Hermione* (1762)

The *Hermione* was an English slave ship that experienced a slave revolt that resulted in the death of several crew members. The slaves were not able to take control of the ship.

- The *Tryal* (1805)

The *Tryal* was a Spanish ship that experienced a mutiny led by an enslaved man named Babo. The result failed, but it was made famous by Herman Melville's novella *Benito Cereno*.

There were other slave mutinies, such as the one on the *Amistad*, which will be talked about later in this book. What is important to understand now is that the humans on board these ships were willing to take significant risks to try to gain their freedom back.

Most slaves who were part of the Atlantic slave trade survived the trip. Of the 12.5 million Africans who crossed the ocean, around 10.7 survived the journey. This still means almost two million lives were lost crossing the Middle Passage. For those who survived, the trauma of the voyage would haunt them for the rest of their lives.

The journey was horrifying, but for most, it was nothing compared to what would happen next. Africans were taken to a foreign shore where they would be subjected to living and working conditions beyond their darkest nightmares.

Chapter 4: African Roots: Societies Uprooted by the Slave Trade

The Atlantic slave trade was a seismic event in the human narrative that upended countless lives and communities. The slave trade had a complex impact on African societies, including social fragmentation and cultural transmission. In reviewing this tragic phenomenon, we have to remember that African rulers and kingdoms were involved, and some were complicit in the trafficking of human beings.

Demographic Devastation

The trade crossed demographic lines. The most significant loss was of healthy young men and women, which resulted in a vacuum in the labor force. That would affect agricultural productivity, cripple artisan industries, and encourage a cycle of poverty and economic stagnation. Laborers desperately needed at home were now somewhere else.

Genetic studies have given us an idea of which parts of West Africa were the most affected. There are four distinct regions where the Atlantic slave trade gathered most of its victims:

- Nigeria (Nigeria)
- Senegambia (The Gambia, Senegal, Guinea-Bissau)
- Coastal West Africa (Sierra Leone, Ghana, Côte d'Ivoire, Liberia)
- Congolese (Angola, Democratic Republic of the Congo).

Ninety-three percent of African Americans and 82 percent of individuals living in the former British and French Caribbean trace their ancestry to these regions. Enslaved women contributed more to the modern gene pool than enslaved men. Caucasian men contributed more than Caucasian women, confirming the sexual violence perpetrated against enslaved women.[27]

Attack on Family Structures

The Atlantic slave trade fractured existing families. Seizing young men and women meant leaving behind children and older people who would now have no support system. Kinship was a valuable part of society in West Africa, but it would splinter as relatives were kidnapped or sold to pay off debts.

Slavery forced changes in the normal lives of people. Women were required to assume unfamiliar roles in labor and social administration. They were now required to not only raise children and perform other tasks women were required to do but also to engage in activities once reserved for men.

Because men were the ones typically sent to the Americas, there was a shortage of males, which resulted in a skewing of the sex ratios and encouraged the remaining men to have multiple wives. Polygyny was already an aspect of many West African societies, but scholars have determined that the Atlantic slave trade caused West Africa to have more instances of polygyny than East Africa.

The Middlemen

Community trust suffered from the involvement of local middlemen in slave raids. There was a network of African traders who captured and brought enslaved Africans from interior regions to European castles and fortresses on the coast. It is argued that Europeans took advantage of preexisting slave trade routes to obtain the labor they needed in the New World.

The idea that West Africa was little more than a jumble of villages and tribes living on subsistence farming is a myth. West Africa had diverse political and social structures that ranged from small states to empires, such as the Empire of Mali or the Songhai Empire. These nations and political entities fought for political and economic

---

[27] Steven J. Mitchell, e. a. (2020, July 23). *Genetic Consequences of the Transatlantic Slave Trade*. Retrieved from AJHG: https://www.cell.com/ajhg/fulltext/S0002-9297(20)30200-7.

objectives.[28]

As mentioned, there were plenty of reasons why Africans decided to collaborate with the European slave traders. There were obvious economic benefits, such as having access to European trade goods. The desire to have European firearms to fight off invading enemies was a solid incentive for selling prisoners of war.

The concept of an African identity was not yet established. African middlemen did not consider the people they enslaved as "their people." Those in bondage were enemies or rivals for whom no pity was expected. Other enslaved people could have been those who had fallen into debt, and the only way out was to sell kin or themselves.

Regardless of the reasons, there were African states that began to center their economy on the slave trade. It was a decision that would have dire consequences hundreds of years later.

BURNING OF A VILLAGE IN AFRICA, AND CAPTURE OF ITS INHABITANTS.

An illustration depicting the burning of a village so the people living there could be sold into slavery.

https://commons.wikimedia.org/wiki/File:Burning_of_a_Village_in_Africa,_and_Capture_of_its_Inhabitants_(p.12,_February_1859,_XVI)_-_Copy.jpg

---

[28] African Passages, Lowcountry Adaptions. (2023, September 25). *Slavery before the Trans-Atlantic Trade*. Retrieved from African Passages, Lowcountry Adaptions: https://ldhi.library.cofc.edu/exhibits/show/africanpassageslowcountryadapt/introductionatlanticworld/slaverybeforetrade.

Social Paranoia

The Atlantic slave trade fueled local enmities among West African communities. The creation of economic incentives, manipulation by Europeans who played one group against the other, and growing demand for even more slaves turned once-friendly neighbors into competitors and allies into enemies.

Tribal distinctions became even more pronounced as communities had to defend themselves from their neighbors who happened to be slave raiders. Animosities were created between groups, some of which still exist to this day. Some communities started to give greater importance to ethnic identity, using that as a criterion for trust and collaboration. The consequence was the solidifying of ethnic divisions.

The slave trade engendered factionalism. People would turn on each other in order to profit from human trafficking. Kidnapping, tricking, and selling each other into slavery became standard practices. Even family members or friends would turn on those who trusted them. This culture of distrust grew stronger as time went on.[29]

Wars over Humans

Slavery became a means to acquire wealth and power. The trade also influenced diplomacy, as disputes that once were settled through negotiation were instead concluded through warfare. With European powers playing one African state against another, nations went to war armed with the weapons the Europeans conveniently provided for them. Let's take a look at some of the most infamous rivalries during this time.

- Wolof people against the Lebou Communities

The Wolof Empire of Senegambia was heavily involved in the slave trade. The need for more Africans to enslave pushed the Wolofs to expand their territorial raids into the fishing communities of the Lebou. The tensions between the two groups grew to a point where trade and intermarriage between them ceased for generations.

- Akan versus Asante

The Asante Empire looked for ways to fill European demands for slaves, and they found it in the Akan community. A cycle followed, and retribution developed, which inflamed historical rivalries and caused

---

[29] Nunn, N. (2017, February 27). *Understanding the Long-run Effects of Africa's Slave Trades.* Retrieved from cepr.org: https://cepr.org/voxeu/columns/understanding-long-run-effects-africas-slave-trades

divisions between the two groups.

- Yoruba Wars

The Oyo Empire was collapsing in the late 18th century, which led to a period of internal strife known as the Yoruba Civil Wars. There were many reasons for the conflicts, but the sale of enslaved people had a significant role in creating the violence. Various Yoruba factions were quick to seize captives from their Oyo rivals, which only added fuel to the fire.

Europeans were doing their best to see to it that warfare continued and that prisoners of war were made available for sale. Nevertheless, it must be understood that innocents did not rule the African kingdoms. The African monarchs developed a craving for European goods and understood their desires were best met by raiding a neighbor and stealing their subjects. Frankly, stiff opposition could have stopped the supply side of the Atlantic slave trade. Some kings did that, but others kept relying on the slave trade to bolster revenue.

The Deeds of Dahomey

The Kingdom of Dahomey was a prominent West African state involved in the Atlantic slave trade from the 17th century to the 19th century. Although European powers bear significant responsibility for initiating and sustaining this trade, Dahomey's role is emblematic of how African polities actively engaged in the slave trade.

European trade goods were appealing to Dahomey's ruling class. Crystals, firearms, and metalware were greatly desired products, and they could be gained by exchanging enslaved people. Consequently, the kingdom's economy became heavily dependent on slavery.

Europeans did business in the kingdom, but they were not allowed to go beyond the main port of Whydah. Only a few were allowed to go into the interior to have an audience with the king. Europeans were not allowed to deal directly with the king's subjects, and the state kept all the profits. The Europeans did not mind this situation since they were ultimately receiving what they wanted.[30]

The Kingdom of Dahomey's close association with the Atlantic slave trade led the kingdom to have diplomatic relations with Brazil, a

---

[30] Saylor.org. (2023, September 25). *The Kingdom of Dahomey*. Retrieved from The Transatlantic Slave Trade:
https://learn.saylor.org/mod/book/view.php?id=54827&chapterid=40411.

Portuguese possession, from 1795 to 1805.

Approximately 4.8 million Africans were transported to Brazil on more than 9,000 voyages during the years of the Atlantic slave trade. Ouidah, an African slave port controlled by Dahomey, delivered over 50 percent of all the enslaved people from the Gulf of Benin region. The primary Brazilian ports of call were Salvador and Rio de Janeiro.

The African kingdom sent two embassies to Brazil with the intention of building close relations with Portuguese colonial authorities and the large slave buyers residing in Brazil. Dahomey wanted to guarantee that it would be the principal supplier of enslaved Africans to Brazil.

The diplomatic missions were not new experiences for the political elite of Dahomey. The kingdom had developed an administrative structure to deal with foreigners, which included accepting embassies at Abomey, the capital of Dahomey. Dahomey employed scribes and translators to facilitate communications.[31]

The Kingdom of Dahomey reached out to other foreign lands besides Brazil. Bulfinche Lamb, a commercial agent for the Royal African Company, delivered a letter from the king of Dahomey to King George I of Great Britain requesting a trade relationship in which guns and gunpowder would be exchanged for slaves.[32]

A Military State

Dahomey's foreign policy was to expand the kingdom by conquest and incorporate smaller kingdoms. Europeans provided the weapons needed to achieve its national goals and objectives. Consequently, Dahomey became a highly militarized state.

The Kingdom of Dahomey had a regiment of women warriors. Their existence is the topic of a recent movie, *The Woman King*, which received a great deal of positive press. What the film does not fully cover, however, is that these ladies were not simply bodyguards to the king. They fought in wars that were conducted for the primary purpose

---

[31] Arantes, J. T. (2021, July 14). *Study Highlights the Role of Diplomatic Relations between Dahomey and Brazil in the Slave Trade.* Retrieved from Agencia FAPESP:
https://agencia.fapesp.br/study-highlights-the-role-of-diplomatic-relations-between-dahomey-and-brazil-in-the-slave-trade/36328.

[32] Historical Society of Pennsylvania. (2008, September 11). *An English Slave Trader, an African Prince & the Pennsylvania Gazette.* Retrieved from Historical Society of Pennsylvania:
https://hsp.org/blogs/hidden-histories/an-english-slave-trader-an-african-prince-the-pennsylvania-gazette.

of producing prisoners to be sold to Brazil and Cuba.[33]

To put it bluntly, Dahomey was not a passive participant in the Atlantic slave trade. Through economic incentives, political machinations, and military force, the Kingdom of Dahomey actively engaged in commerce that had devastating effects on its own society. Moreover, the king's relationships with slave traders were sophisticated enough to have foreign embassies sent and received by the monarch. Dahomey's involvement with the slave trade continued well into the 19th century.

The Cooperation of the Kingdom of Kongo

Kongo was a centralized state in present-day northern Angola and the western Democratic Republic of Congo. It played a pivotal role in the Atlantic slave trade. What began as a friendly, diplomatic, and commercial relationship with the Kingdom of Portugal led to the Kingdom of Kongo becoming increasingly trapped in a spider web.

Human trafficking became a source of revenue for the nation. Kongo imposed taxes on Portuguese merchants and demanded tributes from weaker neighboring states that were partially paid with enslaved people. These practices helped institutionalize the role of slavery within the economy and politics of this African kingdom. Kongo gradually became an integral part of the broader slave trade network.

The Kongolese king initially protected his own subjects who were freeborn. The kingdom was expanding, and there was a steady supply of foreign-born slaves who were the product of various conquests and wars waged against neighboring Ndongo. Most slaves were exported to Portuguese possessions, but the king retained slaves for himself, particularly enslaved criminals. Since the criminals were freeborn Kongolese, they could not be sold to other parties.

The situation changed dramatically within a few years. Portuguese slave traders began kidnapping freeborn Kongolese, including noble children. The problem grew so large that it prompted letters from the king of Kongo, Afonso I, to Portuguese King John III regarding the slave trade. This letter included the following:

---

[33] Araujo, A. L. (2022, September 16). *The Woman King Softens the Truth of the Slave Trade.* Retrieved from Slate.com: https://slate.com/culture/2022/09/woman-king-movie-true-story-dahomey-amazons-slave-trade.html.

"Many of our people, keenly desirous as they are of the wares and things of your Kingdoms, which are brought here by your people, and in order to satisfy their voracious appetite, seize many of our people, freed and exempt men, and very often it happens that they kidnap even noblemen and the sons of noblemen, and our relatives, and take them to be sold to the white men who are in our Kingdoms; and for this purpose they have concealed them; and others are brought during the night so that they might not be recognized.

"And as soon as they are taken by the white men they are immediately ironed and branded with fire, and when they are carried to be embarked, if they are caught by our guards' men the whites allege that they have bought them but they cannot say from whom, so that it is our duty to do justice and to restore to the freemen their freedmen, but it cannot be done if your subjects feel offended, as they claim to be."[34]

Afonso's intent was to end the slave trade, and he asked John III for help.

"That is why we beg of Your Highness to help and assist us in this matter, commanding your factors that they should not send here either merchants or wares, because it is our will that in these Kingdoms there should not be any trade of slaves nor outlet for them. Concerning what is referred [to] above, again we beg of Your Highness to agree with it, since otherwise we cannot remedy such an obvious damage. Pray Our Lord in His mercy to have Your Highness under His guard and let you do forever the things of His service."[35]

Sadly, nothing came of this request. Afonso I was incapable of stopping the slave trade. The elite of Kongo had developed a taste for European goods and ignored all royal requests to help end the slave trade. In 1568, warriors known as the Jaga invaded the Kingdom of Kongo. They were aided by the common people.

Civil wars and internal strife weakened Kongo. By 1710, the central state had collapsed, and the kingdom was carved up among various

---

[34] World History Commons. (2023, September 25). *Excerpt of Letter from Nzinga Mbemba to Portuguese King Jao III*. Retrieved from World History Commons: https://worldhistorycommons.org/excerpt-letter-nzinga-mbemba-portuguese-king-joao-iii#doc_transcription.

[35] Mrcaseyhistory. (2023, September 25). *King Afonso I, Letter to King John III of Portugal*. Retrieved from Mrcaseyhistory.files.wordpress.com: https://mrcaseyhistory.files.wordpress.com/2014/05/king-afonso-i-letter-to-king-john-iii-of-portugal.pdf.

commercial and political interests.[36]

The Kingdom of Kongo's engagement with the Atlantic slave trade was a labyrinth interplay of economic benefits, political realignments, and moral quandaries. Kongo was not an unwitting victim or an enthusiastic collaborator in the slave trade. It was a nation-state that was trying to maneuver through the geopolitical currents of the time. The Atlantic slave trade brought severe pressure on the state and helped to bring about its eventual downfall.

Resistance

Despite the collaboration of some African nations, not all of them engaged in the slave trade. There was resistance to the trade, and people definitely realized what was happening to their communities, neighbors, and families.

Nzinga Mbandi, Queen of Ndongo and Matamba, was a fierce opponent of Portuguese attempts to enslave her people. She used a combination of military action and negotiations to protect her subjects from the slave traders. She worked to end the transportation of enslaved Africans to the Americas. Nzinga also endeavored to free people who were already enslaved. Unfortunately, she was not immune to the lure of slave profits. Nzinga used enslaved people on her plantations and sold prisoners of war to Europeans.[37]

Abdul Kader, Almaami of Futa Toro in modern-day Senegal, is credited with abolishing the slave trade in his territory in the 18th century. This did not mean that his subjects could not enslave people, but European slave traders could not enslave the inhabitants or transport slaves through his territory.

Local attempts to resist the slave trade included the fortification of various towns. One significant difficulty in opposing the slave trade was that taking slaves was ingrained in West African cultures and economies. Once it became established as a source of revenue and profit, the slave trade was very hard to stop. Too many people were making too much money.

---

[36] Mitchell, R. (2023, April 10). *The Rise and Fall of Central Africa's Mighty Kingdom of Kongo*. Retrieved from Ancient Origins: https://www.ancient-origins.net/ancient-places-africa/kingdom-kongo-0018228.

[37] Polat, G. (2023, May 19). *Queen Nzinga: Badass African Queen That Fought the Portuguese & Won*. Retrieved from Trailblazing Women & LGBTQ Folks: https://letherfly.org/queen-nzinga-the-portuguese-sold-her-people-into-slavery-so-she-went-to-war/.

In Summary

It could be argued the Atlantic slave trade tore apart the social fabric of West Africa. Families, communities, and kingdoms gradually broke down as the lust for forced labor grew. Its social implications, including the disintegration of family structures, disruption of gender roles, erosion of community trust, and the weakening of kingdoms, were horrific consequences. It would be generations before any type of sanity was restored to West Africa.

In the meantime, there had to be a way to end the madness. It was going to take outside intervention to finally bring the Atlantic slave trade to an end.

Chapter 5: The Business of Human Trafficking

Slavery was an enterprise where people were merchandise. To sell humans meant stripping people of their dignity. For those in the slave trade business, few cared. They wanted to make sure they could sell enslaved Africans for the best possible price.

A slave ship would eventually dock at the pier of a major slave market, where the process would start to prepare the Africans for auction. The enslaved often were emaciated and sore after the long voyage. Their superficial cuts and bruises were treated, and they were washed. This wasn't to ensure their health or well-being; rather, they were washed to make them look more attractive to a prospective buyer.

The enslaved would be scrubbed to remove the grime and wear from their long journey. Next, they were oiled to give their skin a sheen that made them look healthier than they actually were.

Today, consumer products are labeled; the same was done with slaves. Individuals were seared with symbols or initials of their new owners. Not only was this physically painful, but the enslaved would also bear a lifetime scar that would be a constant reminder of their new status.

The Presentation

A slave about to be auctioned had to look as good as possible. They would be dressed in coarse garments. Clothing could more easily hide sores and other imperfections that might lower a person's value. It is true that many enslaved Africans would be stripped naked for a final inspection, although this did not always happen.

Auction day was a big occasion in the slavery industry. Buyers were willing to spend hundreds or even thousands of dollars on the right person. This meant that enslaved individuals were subjected to meticulous inspections. They would be prodded and probed, their muscles checked for tone, their teeth examined, and their temperament assessed. Families would be separated, with men, women, and children being auctioned off separately.

The physical inspection was part of the presentation. Enslaved people were often made to perform tasks or even tricks to demonstrate their abilities. They would be forced to jump, run, and carry heavy objects. All of this aimed to showcase their vitality and usefulness to prospective customers. Auctioneers often used words such as "specimens" or "units" to emphasize that these human beings were properties to be sold and purchased.

Firsthand Accounts

Formerly enslaved people in 19th-century America left narratives of the experiences they endured in the marketplace. Henry Bibb, in 1849, gave an account that included the pre-sale examination of slaves by inspectors.

"We had there to pass through an examination or inspection by a city officer, whose business it was to inspect slave property that was brought to that Market for sale. He examined our backs to see if we had been much scarred by the lash. He examined our limbs to see whether we were inferior. As it is hard to tell the ages of slaves, they look in their mouths at their teeth and prick up the skin on the back of their hands, and if the person is very far advanced in life, when the skin is pricked up, the pucker will stand so many seconds on the back of the hand. But the most rigorous examinations of slaves by those slave inspectors is on the mental capacity. If they are found to be very intelligent, this is pronounced the most objectionable of all other qualities connected with the life of a slave. In fact, it undermines the whole fabric of his chattelhood; it prepares for what slaveholders are pleased to pronounce the unpardonable sin when committed by a slave. It lays the foundation for running away and going to Canada. They also see in it a love for freedom, patriotism, insurrection, bloodshed, and exterminating war against American slavery. Hence, they are very careful to inquire whether a slave who is for sale can read or write. This question has been asked me often by slave traders and cotton planters, while I was there for market. After conversing with me, they have sworn by their Maker that they would not have me among their negroes and that they saw the devil in my eye; I would run away, &c [etc.]."[38]

In an 1858 account, Josiah Henson tells of how his family was separated at a slave auction.

"My brothers and sisters were bid off first, and one by one, while my mother, paralyzed by grief, held me by the hand. Her turn came, and she was bought by Isaac Riley of Montgomery County. Then I was offered to the assembled purchasers. My mother, half distracted with the thought of parting forever from all her children, pushed through the crowd while the bidding for me was going on, to the spot where Riley was standing. She fell at his feet and clung to his knees, entreating him in tones that a mother only could command to buy her baby as well as herself, and spare to her one, at least, of her little ones. Will it, can it, be believed that this man, thus appealed to, was capable not merely of turning a deaf ear to her supplication, but of disengaging himself from her with such violent blows and kicks as to reduce her to the necessity of creeping out of his reach and mingling the groan of bodily suffering with the sob of a breaking heart? As she crawled away from the brutal man, I heard her sob out, 'Oh, Lord Jesus, how long, how long shall I suffer this way!; I must have been then between five and six years old. I seem to see and hear my poor weeping mother now."[39]

Henson never saw his siblings again.

William Wells Brown was hired out by his master to help transport slaves down the Mississippi River. In 1849, he recounts what he saw while shipping human cargo to New Orleans.

"There was on the boat a large room on the lower deck, in which the slaves were kept, men and women, promiscuously–all chained two and two, and a strict watch kept that they did not get loose; for cases have occurred in which slaves have got off their chains, and made their escape at landing-places while the boats were taking in wood – and with all our care, we lost one woman who had been taken from her husband and children, and having no desire to live without them, in the agony of her soul jumped overboard and drowned herself. She was not chained. It

---

[38] Bibb, H. Chapter IX. https://pressbooks.library.torontomu.ca/henrybibb/chapter/9/.

[39] Henson, J. *Truth Stanger than Fiction*. https://docsouth.unc.edu/neh/henson58/henson58.html.

was almost impossible to keep that part of the boat clean. On landing at Natchez, the slaves were all carried to the slave-pen and there kept one week, during which time several of them were sold. Mr. Walker fed his slaves well. We took on board, at St. Louis, several hundred pounds of bacon (smoked meat) and cornmeal, and his slaves were better fed than slaves generally were in Natchez, so far as my observation extended. At the end of a week, we left for New Orleans, the place of our final destination, which we reached in two days. Here the slaves were placed in a negro-pen, where those who wished to purchase could call and examine them. The negro-pen is a small yard, surrounded by buildings, from fifteen to twenty feet wide, with the exception of a large gate with iron bars. The slaves are kept in the buildings during the night and turned out into the yard during the day. After the best of the stock was sold at private sale at the pen, the balance were taken to the Exchange Coffee House Auction Rooms, kept by Isaac L. McCoy, and sold at public auction. After the sale of this lot of slaves, we left New Orleans for St. Louis."[40]

Slave auctions might also include elderly people. They were at considerable risk because they did not have the physical strength to do hard manual labor. William Wells Brown writes about how they were prepared for the market.

"In the course of eight or nine weeks, Mr. Walker had his cargo of human flesh made up. There was in this lot a number of old men and women, some of them with gray locks. We left St. Louis in the steamboat Carlton, Captain Swan, bound for New Orleans. On our way down, and before we reached Rodney, the place where we made our first stop, I had to prepare the old slaves for market. I was ordered to have the old men's whiskers shaved off and the grey hairs plucked out, where they were not too numerous, in which case he had a preparation of blacking to color it, and with a blacking-brush we would put it on. This was new business to me and was performed in a room where the passengers could not see us. These slaves were also taught how old they were by Mr. Walker, and after going through the blacking process, they looked ten or fifteen years younger; and I am sure that some of those who purchased slaves of Mr. Walker were dreadfully cheated, especially

---

[40] Brown, William. *Narrative of William W. Brown.* https://docsouth.unc.edu/neh/brown47/brown47.html.

in the ages of the slaves which they bought."[41]

Those elderly slaves who were not sold might have been forced to live in extreme neglect without adequate food, shelter, or medical care. They were viewed as too much of a burden and might have been killed to avoid any further expense in keeping them alive.[42]

The Marketplace

There were marketplaces that stood out in the New World. These were shaped by local economic demands, colonial policies, and cultural practices, but what they had in common was the sale of enslaved humans. The volume of several of these markets was measured in tens of thousands. Their peak volumes often happened after the slave trade was formally abolished.

- Rio de Janeiro

Rio de Janeiro was a critical port city with a thriving economy due mainly to sugar plantations and coffee estates. The immense demand for labor made Rio de Janeiro a prime destination for slavers.

Valongo Wharf is a World Heritage Site and was a primary landing point for enslaved people. The wharf was essentially a complex consisting of various parts, including holding areas known as lazarettos. The death rate in these holding pens was incredibly high because of disease, malnutrition, and brutal treatment.

The Valongo Wharf Archaeological Site takes up all of the Jornal do Comércio Square. The site is composed of several archaeological layers, the lowest of which consists of floor pavings that are attributed to the original wharf.

The entire area was a bustling center of commercial activity. Brazil was the largest importer of enslaved people in the Americas. An estimated 900,000 Africans came through the Valongo Wharf alone.[43]

---

[41] Brown, William. *Narrative of William W. Brown*.
https://docsouth.unc.edu/neh/brown47/brown47.html.

[42] National Humanities Center. (2023, September 18). *Slave Auctions*. Retrieved from Nationalhumanitiescener.org:
https://nationalhumanitiescenter.org/pds/maai/enslavement/text2/slaveauctions.pdf.

[43] Lodi, C. (2023, September 18). *Washing of the Valongo Wharf, Rio de Janeiro (Brazil)*. Retrieved from Whc.unesco.org: https://whc.unesco.org/en/canopy/valongo/.

- The Port of Havana

Havana was vital to the Atlantic slave trade due to its geographic location and economic significance. The harbor was among the most secure and navigable in the Caribbean, making it an attractive port of entry for slave ships arriving from Africa. Havana was not just the port of entry for the Cuban slave trade. It was a hub for other parts of the Caribbean and mainland Latin America.

Spanish Cuba relied heavily on sugar plantations, which needed massive numbers of laborers. The indigenous population was almost wiped out due to disease and exploitation, making enslaved Africans the primary labor source. Somewhere between ten thousand to twenty thousand African slaves were sold annually in Havana. The port was incredibly busy.

Slaves were placed in hold pens called barracoons, where they were readied for auction. These were cramped and disease-ridden spaces where enslaved people were subject to appalling conditions. The enslaved would be covered in chalk or lard to hide physical blemishes or scars.

Population demographics give a better appreciation of how significant the slave trade was for Cuba. Between 1763 and 1860, Cuba's population went from less than 150,000 people to more than 1,300,000. The slave population increased from 39,000 in the 1770s to nearly 400,000 in the 1840s, meaning that roughly one-third of the island's population was enslaved people in the mid-19th century.

The slave population grew even larger during the 19th century, as Cuba imported more than 600,000 slaves. Most of those people arrived after 1820, the year when Spain and Great Britain agreed to end the slave trade in Spanish colonies.[44]

- Bridgetown, Barbados

Barbados was a jewel in the British Empire's crown. It had fertile soil that was ideal for sugar cultivation and held the promise of considerable profits. As mentioned, growing sugarcane and processing sugar is a very labor-intensive industry and requires considerable human effort. Consequently, Barbados became a hub for slave activity. Bridgetown had one of the most active slave markets in the Caribbean.

---

[44] Britannica.com. (2023, September 19). *Sugarcane and the Growth of Slavery*. Retrieved from Britannica.com: https://www.britannica.com/place/Cuba/Sugarcane-and-the-growth-of-slavery.

Interestingly, the planters initially used white laborers as indentured servants to work on the farms. This was the result of the English Civil War. Irish prisoners were sent to Barbados. These fair-skinned laborers succumbed to the heat and were gradually replaced by African slaves.

By 1684, there were approximately 46,500 African slaves and 19,500 white Europeans on the island. The export of enslaved Africans to Barbados was expedited by the creation of the Royal African Company in 1672. This enterprise was protected by the Royal Navy. The duke of York, who later became King James II of Great Britain, was a principal of the company.

Slave auctions in Bridgetown were an open affair and publicly staged. These commercial meetings attracted crowds of planters, settlers, and merchants.

The oppressive treatment of enslaved people was made a part of the law in 1661 when the planters of Barbados passed the Barbados Slave Code. This code described Africans as a dangerous kind of people and permitted violent punishments for any offenses.[45]

- Charleston, South Carolina

Great Britain's North American colonies became more profitable as the 17th century progressed. South Carolina's rice, indigo, and cotton plantations made this colony rich. Forced labor was seen as necessary for cultivation, and Charleston became a primary port for the Atlantic slave trade.

Between 1670 and 1808, nearly one thousand cargoes of enslaved Africans entered Charleston. That translates into approximately 150,200 slaves. Charleston was the receiving port for more slaves than any other port in mainland North America.[46]

Charleston had various sites where the buying and selling of enslaved people happened. The Old Exchange Building was the place where open-air auctions were held. A city ordinance was eventually passed to prohibit the practice of public sales, and the transactions needed to go

---

[45] Abdul Mohamud, R. W. (2018, June 21). *Britain's Involvement with the New World: Slavery and the Transatlantic Slave Trade*. Retrieved from Bl.uk: https://www.bl.uk/restoration-18th-century-literature/articles/britains-involvement-with-new-world-slavery-and-the-transatlantic-slave-trade.

[46] Charleston County Public Library. (2023, September 18). *Nearly 1,000 Cargos: The Legacy of Importing Africans into Charleston*. Retrieved from Charleston County Public Library: https://www.ccpl.org/charleston-time-machine/nearly-1000-cargos-legacy-importing-africans-charleston.

inside. The Old Slave Mart, formerly Ryan's Mart, is the only known slave auction building still in existence in South Carolina. It was opened in 1856, along with other indoor sales rooms that could be found along State, Queen, and Chalmers Streets.

The Old Slave Mart was part of a complex of buildings and consisted of a yard enclosed by a high brick wall, a four-story barracoon, a slave jail, a kitchen, and a morgue. The last slave auction took place in November 1863.[47]

The Preservation of Sites

It would be easy to allow urban progress and buildings to cover all of the places where slaves were bought and sold. However, that has not happened. Brazil has invested considerable time and money into the care and preservation of the Valongo Wharf, which holds particular significance to the African Brazilian community.

The site of the Old Slave Mart in Charleston was once used as an auto repair shop. It was made into a museum in 1938 and was placed on the National Register of Historic Places in 1973. Charleston acquired the property in 1988, and the site was opened as a historic site and museum in 2007.

Barbados has inaugurated the Barbados Heritage District. Situated on the grounds of what was once the Newton Plantation, the district will include the Newton Enslaved Burial Ground Memorial to commemorate the remains of 570 enslaved people buried in unmarked graves on the property.

Rules in Place

Of course, the consequences of the Atlantic slave trade did not end when the auctioneer's gavel came down. The enslaved were transferred to plantations, mines, households, or other places where they would be put to work, often under very harsh conditions. The planters were effectively the law of the land on most Caribbean islands. Their money and influence permitted them to enact legislation that made their slaves less than human in the eyes of the law.

The power of the plantation elite essentially put them beyond the reach of the law. There were rules in place for the treatment of slaves, but considerable exceptions were made for those who owned

---

[47] Charleston SC. (2023, September 19). *Old Slave Mart Museum.* Retrieved from Chaleston-sc.gov: https://www.charleston-sc.gov/160/Old-Slave-Mart-Museum.

plantations. These commercial aristocrats could do practically whatever they pleased on the land they owned.

Admittedly, some of them were decent people. There is evidence of that. There were patricians who were sensitive to the needs of their slaves. Nevertheless, good or bad, plantation owners held absolute power and subjugated other human beings. Their dominance would corrupt absolutely.

Chapter 6: Plantation System in the New World

Slaves were forced to work in mines and households, but most enslaved Africans were sent to work on plantations. Most of the profits generated by the New World, outside of gold and silver mining, came from plantations that cultivated sugar, tobacco, indigo, rice, or coffee. The hours were long, the working conditions were incredibly harsh, and basic human rights were ignored.

The planters ruled supreme on the land they owned, and the slaves existed to generate money for them. The respective colonial powers influenced the conditions on the plantations. What a slave was subjected to often depended on the sovereign flag flying over the land, although there were themes common to all enslaved in the Americas.

Working and Living Conditions

It is a given that slaves were expected to work long days full of hard labor. Here is a look at what the enslaved could expect in different places in the Americas.

- Cuba

Slavery in Cuba was deeply entwined with the rise of the sugar plantation economy, which was the cornerstone of the island's colonial history. The *ingenio* system was practiced in Cuba and was centered on the large sugar mills, *ingenios*, which were the center of the sugar industry. The *ingenios* were industrial sites consisting of fields, factories, and living quarters for slaves.

A tiered system arose in which slaves were subjected to various levels of hardship and surveillance. There were skilled labor jobs, but the slaves were primarily employed in dangerous tasks, such as grinding sugarcane.

People were crowded into confined spaces for sleeping and were under constant surveillance. A slave was often separated from family members and could be deprived of privacy.

- Brazil

In Brazil, the enslaved were engaged in tasks such as planting, cutting, hauling, and processing sugarcane. Brazil had a daily work quota, the *tarefa*, that each slave was expected to fulfill. Failure to meet these daily quotas would result in harsh punishments. The *tarefas* were often set at unrealistically high figures to keep slaves working at maximum capacity.

- French Caribbean

A hierarchy existed on the French sugar plantations. Slaves were divided into field slaves, domestic slaves, and artisan slaves. Each endured different types of abuse. Field slaves worked from sunrise to sunset, laboring under the hot sun and the close eye of overseers who would use violence to ensure the enslaved were working as hard as they could. Domestic slaves and artisan slaves were not involved with fieldwork but lived close to their masters, which made them more vulnerable to physical and sexual abuse.

- British Caribbean

The British practiced a systematic form of abuse toward the enslaved. Newly arrived slaves often went through a process of "seasoning" that was meant to break their spirits. It typically included harsh labor, poor nutrition, and psychological abuse. What made the British seasoning system stand out were the detailed ledgers and accounts of what the masters did to acclimate their property to plantation slavery.

The British practiced a driver system in which selected slaves were appointed as drivers to oversee the work of other slaves. This created a hierarchy within the slave population that pitted one group of slaves against another.

- South Carolina

South Carolina plantations would employ task systems to organize labor. The enslaved were assigned specific tasks to complete each day. Once those tasks were completed, slaves could work in their gardens or engage in other activities.

Legal Codes

The colonial powers in the New World established laws and regulations regarding slaves and the practice of slavery. These statutes often covered more than the terms and conditions of a person's servitude.

Código Negro

Spanish law in the 16th and 17th centuries permitted enslaved people to have certain rights. These included the right to purchase their freedom and access to Catholic sacraments. In 1789, the Spanish Crown sought to reform slavery in response to the growing demand for forced labor. The Código Negro Español was a royal decree that specified quotas for slaves, limited the number of work hours, limited punishments, required religious instruction, and protected marriages. The Código Negro also forbade the sale of young children if it separated them from their mothers. The decree was not always followed by the planters, who saw it as a threat to their authority.

Brazil had laws that permitted the manumission of slaves either through self-purchase or as a reward for service. The Law of the Free Womb, enacted in 1871, had particular importance. It declared that all children born to enslaved women would be free, although they had to work for their parents' owner until they were adults. This law was circumvented by birth certificates being deliberately forged to prove that the child was born before the law was passed. A law created in 1885, the Saraiva-Cotegipe Law, mandated that enslaved people over sixty years of age would be freed. However, the law also permitted owners to abandon those older people once they became less productive.[48]

French Caribbean

Louis XIV issued a decree in 1685 that guided France's slavery policy until 1789. The Code Noir stipulated that all slaves would be instructed as Catholics and defined the condition of slavery (for instance, slavery passed through the mother, not the father). Harsh controls were levied on slaves (e.g., striking a master or member of the master's family resulted in execution, and fugitive slaves could lose their ears). The enslaved had virtually no rights, although masters were urged to take care

---

[48] The Brazilian Report. (2020, May 13). *Slavery in Brazil*. Retrieved from Wilsoncenter.org: https://www.wilsoncenter.org/blog-post/slavery-brazil.

of the sick and old.[49]

Great Britain

Great Britain provided the most restrictive laws regarding enslaved people in the New World. There was the Barbados Slave Code of 1661 and the later Slave Code of 1667, which included amendments to the original.

The racism in the language of these codes is breathtaking. Enslaved Africans were referred to as "heathenish, brutish, and an uncertain, dangerous kind of people." Punishments were severe. One penalty for striking a master stands out:

"Hee shall bee severely whipped and be burned in the face. For the third offense, he shall receive by order of the Governor and Council such greater corporal punishment as they shall think meet to inflict provided always that such striking or conflict be not in the lawful defense of their Master, Mistress or owners of their Families or of their goods."[50]

The Barbados Slave Code was a model for other British possessions in the New World. South Carolina enacted comparable legislation that gave maximum control to the slaveholders and denied fundamental human rights to anyone who was enslaved.

Sexual Abuse

Since enslaved women and men were seen as property, many instances of sexual abuse took place. Rape was commonplace, especially among women. Children born from such violence might also be enslaved depending on the colonial power in charge. There were instances where slaves were forced to produce offspring to increase the number of slaves. These children could be sold unless the law expressly prohibited it.

Slave Rebellions

People can only take so much abuse before they finally have enough and rebel. Working conditions on plantations were routinely terrible. Life expectancy was very low on a sugar plantation, and the annual mortality rate was high.

---

[49] Liberte, Egalite, Fraternite. (2023, October 1). *The Code Noir (The Blak Code)*. Retrieved from Revolution.chnm.org: https://revolution.chnm.org/d/335/.
[50] SLP. (2023, October 1). *Barbados Slave Code (1661-1667)*. Retrieved from Slaverylawpower.org: https://slaverylawpower.org/barbados-slave-code/.

For most enslaved people, they had little to lose but a lot to gain. Slave uprisings were common in the Americas, and some of them were incredibly violent. Several rebellions have a special significance in the history of the Atlantic slave trade.

The Maroon Wars (1728-1740)

Great Britain seized control of Jamaica from the Spanish in 1655 and instituted its own harsher version of slavery. What the British did not realize was that Jamaica had a population of runaway slaves who found refuge in the mountains of the interior. They were known as the Maroons.

Maroon is derived from the Spanish word "Cimmarrones," which means fierce or unruly. They were free people who resisted the Spanish for years. At first, the British got along well with the Maroons and entered in an alliance with them to force the remaining Spanish to leave the island. However, tensions grew when the British tried to dislodge the Maroons from their mountain fortresses.

Warfare erupted in 1720 when the Maroons began raiding British plantations along the base of the mountains. In 1728, the British escalated matters by sending more troops to Jamaica.

The Maroons used the mountainous terrain to their advantage. There were two groups: the Windward Maroons, who were led by a man named Captain Quao, and the Leeward Maroons, led by a guerrilla warfare genius named Cudjoe.

The British were unable to defeat the Maroons and decided to end the conflict through negotiation. The Leeward and Windward Treaties of 1739 ended the wars. However, slavery still existed in Jamaica, and the treaties required the Maroons to return runaway slaves to the British.

Nevertheless, the conflict showed that the British were not the complete masters of their Caribbean possessions. A well-organized and well-led opposition could make significant inroads.[51]

The Haitian Revolution (1791-1804)

The Haitian Revolution has been called the largest and most successful slave rebellion in world history. The Haitian Revolution ended with the creation of the Republic of Haiti, the first government in the Americas that formerly enslaved people controlled.

---

[51] Maroon History. (2023, October 1). *Maroon History*. Retrieved from Cyber.harvard.edu: https://cyber.harvard.edu/eon/maroon/history.html.

Saint-Domingue was a source of immense wealth for France, generating more revenue than all of the British North American colonies combined. Sugar, coffee, indigo, and cotton were staples, and they produced staggering profits. Slaves provided the labor.

Saint-Domingue had five interest groups in the later years of the 18th century:

- White planters: They were the ones who owned the plantations and slaves.
- Petit Blancs: They were shopkeepers, artisans, and teachers. Most did not own slaves, although some did.
- Free Blacks: Not every person of color was enslaved. There were free black people in Saint-Domingue. Approximately 50 percent were mulattos and were, by and large, wealthier than the Petit Blancs.
- Slaves: They worked the fields, processed the sugar, and performed the hard labor that made Saint-Domingue a treasure for the French.
- Maroons: They were runaway slaves who lived deep in the mountains and survived by subsistence farming.

The white planters and the Petit Blancs in the 1780s numbered about forty thousand people. There were approximately thirty thousand free blacks. There was no way to estimate how many Maroons there were. There were nearly 500,000 enslaved people, though. They outnumbered whites by a ratio of over ten to one.[52]

The French Revolution

The white planters did their best to keep things under control, but there were slave rebellions throughout the history of the French colony. The situation became radically different with the French Revolution. White planters from Saint-Domingue went to France and demanded representation in the National Assembly. They did not expect the reaction they received from Paris. There were deputies of the National Assembly who were members of the Society of the Friends of Blacks who advocated for the abolition of the slave trade and argued for full civil rights to be granted to all free blacks in the colonies. There was a

---

[52] Sutherland, C. (2007, July 16). *Haitian Revolution (1791-1804)*. Retrieved from BlackPast: https://www.blackpast.org/global-african-history/haitian-revolution-1791-1804/.

significant cry in Paris for the abolition of slavery.[53]

In March 1790, the French National Assembly approved the Declaration of the Rights of Man and of the Citizen. This monumental document, which espoused the inherent rights of men, paved the way for the passage of a law in 1791 that granted citizenship to free people of color who were born of two free parents. This law was not acceptable to the white planters and increased friction and turmoil in the French colony.

Finally, on August 22nd, 1791, the slaves revolted and took possession of the northern province of the colony. Three prominent leaders of the rebellion began to emerge: Toussaint Louverture, Jean-Jacques Dessalines, and Henri Christophe. Léger-Félicité Sonthonax, a delegate sent by the French government, declared an end to slavery effective August 29th, 1793.[54]

Louverture eventually gained control of large portions of Saint-Domingue. He proclaimed himself governor-general for life in January 1801. Napoleon Bonaparte tried to regain control of Saint-Domingue and sent an expeditionary force to the island. Louverture was imprisoned by the French and died on April 7th, 1803.

Meanwhile, Dessalines and Christophe fought the French, who were decimated by yellow fever. Ultimately, with the help of the British Royal Navy, the French were defeated, and Saint-Domingue, now known as Haiti, was declared independent on January 1st, 1804.[55]

---

[53] Liberte, Egalite, raternte. (2023, October 1). *Slavery and the Haitian Revolution.* Retrieved from Revolution.chrm.org: https://revolution.chnm.org/exhibits/show/liberty--equality--fraternity/slavery-and-the-haitian-revolu.

[54] Bradshaw, J. (2023, October 1). *Saint-Domingue Revolution.* Retrieved from 64 Parishes: https://64parishes.org/entry/saint-domingue-revolution?gclid=EAIaIQobChMIztKF2JqtgQMVRA6zAB1uKgxcEAAYAiAAEgL9sPD_BwE.

[55] Britannica.com. (2023, October 1). *Haitian Revolution.* Retrieved from Britannica.com: https://www.britannica.com/topic/Haitian-Revolution.

Toussaint Louverture.
https://commons.wikimedia.org/wiki/File:G%C3%A9n%C3%A9ral_Toussaint_Louverture.jpg

The Haitian Revolution had far-reaching consequences for the Atlantic slave trade. It was the first time that a slave uprising in the Americas had succeeded, and it was the first slave uprising in history that established an independent nation. The Haitian Revolution inspired everyone who wanted to end slavery in the New World, and it fueled activities that led to the abolition of the institution.

Bussa's Rebellion (1816)

The British Empire was not immune from slave uprisings. Rebellion was in the air, and discontent was spreading through the islands. Barbados had its share of slave uprisings in earlier years, but a significant rebellion occurred on April 14th, 1816. It was the largest slave uprising in the history of Barbados.

Led by a man named Bussa, slaves rose up in St. Philip Parish and set the sugarcane fields on fire. More than seventy estates were severely damaged. Martial law was declared on April 15th, and a combination of local militia and British imperial troops suppressed the riot. More than two hundred rebels were executed for their actions.[56]

The Demerara Rebellion (1823)

Although the transatlantic slave trade was outlawed by Great Britain in 1807, slavery was still used in its colonies. British Guiana, present-day Guyana, had a reputation for its inhumane treatment of the enslaved. People would perform backbreaking labor under the hot sun and be whipped if they moved too slow or spoke out of turn.

Jack Gladstone led a rebellion in August 1823. It eventually involved thirteen thousand slaves on sixty plantations. On August 20th, two hundred slaves were killed by British soldiers who were ordered to open fire on two thousand rebels who would not disperse. Reprisals, such as torture, followed, and the rebellion was crushed.[57]

The slave rebellions in the British colonies continued; for instance, there would be a significant uprising in Jamaica in 1831. These were all eventually put down, but the British newspapers were not silent about the destruction and the killing.

Public opinion once had a laissez-faire attitude toward slavery, but such nonchalance was rapidly fading. Trafficking humans was no longer viewed as a worthwhile or moral enterprise, and many people began demanding an end to it. The days of an active Atlantic slave trade were numbered.

---

[56] Momdou, S. (2017, August 13). *Bussa Rebellion (1816)*. Retrieved from BlackPast: https://www.blackpast.org/global-african-history/bussa-rebellion-1816/#:~:text=The%20rebellion%20took%20its%20name,by%20the%20British%20in%201838.

[57] Lashmar, J. S. (2023, August 19). *A Huge Human Drama: How the Revolt That Began on the Gladstone Plantation Led to Emancipation*. Retrieved from Theguardian.com: https://www.theguardian.com/world/2023/aug/19/how-revolt-gladstone-plantation-led-to-emancipation-demerara-rebellion.

Chapter 7: The Human Toll of the Slave Trade

The Atlantic slave trade indelibly marked the lives of millions, and it altered the trajectory of entire continents. To quantify the horror of this enterprise is to engage in an exercise of absurdity; numbers and statistics cannot fully capture the scope of human suffering brought about by the slave trade.

Yet, understanding the depth of its impact—physically, psychologically, and emotionally—on enslaved people and their families is critical to fully understanding what happened. The human toll of the slave trade is not an abstract concept but rather a reality that remains in modern society's collective memory. Personal accounts and oral histories allow us to take a deeper look.

Physical Impact: Forced Labor and Squalid Conditions

We have talked about the working conditions the enslaved faced previously in the book. An enslaved person's day often started at sunrise and ended at sundown. There were times, especially during the harvest and when the sugar had to be processed, that the work hours extended late into the evening. The slaves were fortunate if they were able to get Sundays and a few holidays off.

Enslaved people were subjected to an array of physically demanding tasks depending on regional needs and the crops grown there. In the Caribbean and the American South, slaves primarily worked on sugarcane, cotton, indigo, or rice plantations.

The work in the sugarcane fields was particularly brutal. Cutting sugarcane required sharp instruments and a great deal of physical strength. Repetitive motions under the hot sun, often for twelve to sixteen hours a day, led to a multitude of physical ailments like heat exhaustion, severe dehydration, and cuts that could quickly become infected.

Slaves on cotton plantations faced backbreaking work as well. Picking cotton involves stooping or squatting for extended periods, leading to debilitating back problems. The cotton plants themselves have sharp spines that often cut the hands of people picking them, which could result in wounds and subsequent infections.

A slave's diet was often insufficient in both quantity and quality, leading to diseases such as scurvy, rickets, and pellagra. The impact of malnutrition was further exacerbated by parasites and intestinal diseases, which were prevalent due to poor sanitation.

Healthcare for enslaved people was not a priority for slaveholders. Many enslaved people relied on folk remedies or were left to fend for themselves. When medical treatment was provided, it was often administered by other slaves with limited resources rather than by trained medical professionals.

The Tale of the Bones

Spanish Mexico initially relied on indigenous people to toil in the mines and tend the crops. As the indigenous population decreased, Africans were imported to the Viceroyalty of New Spain. Between 130,000 and 150,000 Africans were estimated to be imported before slave imports were banned in 1779.

The cemeteries tell the tale of the physical abuse and hardship endured by the enslaved. In 1992, during the excavations for a new subway line in downtown Mexico City, a mass grave was uncovered that contained skeletal remains of enslaved people. The remains of three individuals whose dental modification patterns reflected those found in different African cultural practices were specifically analyzed for anthropological studies.

These individuals lived from 1436 to 1626, according to radiocarbon dating. Genetic testing suggests they were from southern or western Africa. Their bones reveal lives filled with severe hardship.

The first showed abnormal skeletal changes that are often in response to conditions associated with diet, such as anemia and malnutrition, as well as parasitic infections. Dental health revealed signs of periodontal disease, and the bones in his legs appear to have been broken and then reformed. Clinical testing showed new bone development that might have resulted from microtrauma associated with repetitive use and ordinarily found among people who carry heavy loads on their shoulders. Discs in the spine were protruded due to compression.

The second skeleton showed periodontitis and signs of bones that were broken and fractured and then healed. Degenerative diseases had damaged his joints. There was evidence of a machete wound in the skull and skeletal changes that resulted from intense and gradual compression on the spinal discs.

The third had lesions on his skull, which could have been caused by malnutrition or anemia, parasitic infections, loss of blood, or peritonitis. The bones had been broken and then reformed. There was evidence of infections in the long bones of his body and a series of skull and leg fractures.[58]

Personal Narratives of Physical Cruelty

Formerly enslaved people were encouraged in the 19th century to write accounts of how they had been treated while enslaved. Solomon Northup penned his narrative, *Twelve Years a Slave: Narrative of Solomon Northup, a Citizen of New-York, Kidnapped in Washington City in 1841, and Rescued in 1853*, in 1853. He mentions the torture he endured when his kidnappers used physical violence to break his spirit.

"As soon as these formidable whips appeared, I was seized by both of them, and roughly divested of my clothing. My feet, as has been stated, were fastened to the floor ... With the paddle, Burch commenced beating me. Blow after blow was inflicted on my naked body. When his unrelenting arm grew tired, he stopped and asked if I still insisted I was a free man. I did insist upon it, and then the blows were renewed, faster and more energetically, if possible, than before."[59]

Cruelty was a means by which slaveholders held control over their slaves. Frederick Douglass, one of the most well-known American

---

[58] Rogers, K. (2020, April 30). *The Personal Stories of 3 Enslaved Africans, as Told by Their Bones*. Retrieved from Cnn.com: https://www.cnn.com/2020/04/30/world/enslaved-african-history-trans-atlantic-slave-trade-trnd-scn/index.html.
[59] Lieblich, M. (2023, September 25). *The Cultural Significance of Solomon Northup's Twelve Years a Slave*. Retrieved from U.S. History Scene: https://ushistoryscene.com/article/12-years-a-slave/.

abolitionists and writers who had been born into slavery, explained the significance of physical violence for the enslaved and slave owners.

"But the slave must be brutalized to keep him as a slave. The slaveholder feels this necessity. I admit this necessity … The whip, the chain, the gag, the thumb-screw, the blood-hound, the stocks, and all the other bloody paraphernalia of the slave system, are indispensably necessary to the relation of master and slave. The slave must be subjected to these, or he ceases to be a slave … [Let him know] that his master's authority over him is no longer to be enforced by taking his life—and immediately he walks out from the house of bondage and asserts his freedom as a man."[60]

Brutality was common to the point of being casual. Bill Collins, an Alabama slave who was born in 1846, recollected his own experiences with his master.

"My master was so cruel to his slaves that they were almost crazy at times. He would buckle us across a log and whip us until we were unable to walk for three days. On Sunday, we would go to the barn and pray to God to fix some way for us to be freed from our mean masters."[61]

Psychological Assaults

The slave trade's legacy is often reduced to its physical toll, overshadowing its equally devastating psychological impacts. The brutality slaves suffered was not merely physical but also mental and emotional, leaving psychological scars that would last lifetimes and even cross generations.

The process of dehumanization began with a person's capture. Each transaction, auction, and whipping served as a reminder of an enslaved person's supposed "non-human" status. The internalized dehumanization manifested in various psychological disorders, some of which were akin to what is now termed complex post-traumatic stress disorder (CPTSD).

---

[60] Choi, M. (2023, September 25). *Necessary Violence in Frederick Douglass's Narrative.* Retrieved from Methodist.edu: https://www.methodist.edu/wp-content/uploads/2022/06/mr2020_choi.pdf

[61] Morris, G. (2017, July 1). *Unspeakable Cruelty: Former Slaves Tell Their Stories in Southern University Online Listings.* Retrieved from The Advocate: https://www.theadvocate.com/baton_rouge/entertainment_life/unspeakable-cruelty-former-slaves-tell-their-stories-in-southern-university-online-listings/article_996926ae-579c-11e7-9d36-13d23afca32d.html

Stories from the Crossing

Being captured from one's home was terrifying. These people were ripped from their homes and families and then placed in a slave-holding prison. That kind of thing remained in a person's psyche for the rest of their lives. Ajayi, a Yoruba, gives a detailed account of how slave raiders seized him.

"The morning in which my town, Ocho-gu, shared the same fate which many others had experienced, was fair and delightful and most of the inhabitants were engaged in their respective occupations. We were preparing breakfast without any apprehension when, about 9 o'clock am a rumor was spread in the town, that the enemies had approached with the intention of hostility.

"Here, a most sorrowful scene imaginable was to be witnessed! Women, some with three, four or six children clinging to their arms, with infants on their backs, and such baggage as they could carry on their heads, running as fast as they could through prickly shrubs, which hooking their blies and other loads, drew them down from the heads of the bearers. While they found it impossible to go along with loads, they endeavored only to save themselves and their children: even this was impracticable with those who had many children to care for."[62]

Personal narratives of the Middle Passage crossings are particularly horrifying. The eyewitness accounts of what was happening below decks show the degradation human beings who were bound for slavery faced.

Asa-Asa, who eventually ended up in the French West Indies, spoke of the conditions he encountered when he was placed in the hold of a slave ship.

"The slaves we saw on board the ship were chained together by the legs below deck, so close they could not move. They were flogged very cruelly. I saw one of them flogged till he died; we could not tell what for. They gave them enough to eat. The place they were confined in below deck was so hot and nasty I could not bear to be in it. A great many of the slaves were ill, but they were not attended to. They used to flog me very bad on board the ship: the captain cut my head very bad one

---

[62] Middle Passage Ceremonies and Port Markers Project (MPCPMP). (2012, January 11). *Personal Stories of Captured Africans*. Retrieved from Middle Passage Ceremonies and Port Markers Project (MPCPMP): https://www.middlepassageproject.org/2012/01/11/personal-stories-of-captured-africans/.

time."[63]

The Auction Block

The assault on the psyche of an enslaved person continued after the slave ship reached the harbor. After being sold, enslaved people were often branded and renamed, thus erasing their identities and reinforcing their status as property. (A fictionalized yet famous example of this comes from the television series *Roots*, in which Kunta Kinte is renamed Toby.). The loss of their name and the infliction of a brand served as a psychological anchor of their dehumanized status, creating a sense of existential void and erasure of personhood.

The trauma of the auction block came next. Families were often torn apart. The psychological impact of being separated was monumental. Parents lived with the constant dread of losing children, and children grew up in fractured families, affecting their psychological well-being and understanding of familial bonds.

Mental Health Breakdowns and Suicide

Accounts of formerly enslaved people mention instances of suicidal thoughts and attempts among the enslaved to kill themselves, pointing to a mental health crisis that could not be openly addressed or treated. Suicide was a means of escape from a brutal reality. The Works Progress Administration (WPA) in the 1930s interviewed formerly enslaved people about their days of bondage. Suicide was a common topic of conversation.

Martin Jackson told WPA interviewers of the suicide of a family member:

"My mother was drowned years before when I was a little boy. I only remember her after she was dead. I can take you to the spot in the river today where she was drowned. She drowned herself. I never knew the reason behind it, but it was said she started to lose her mind and preferred death to that."[64]

---

[63] Middle Passage Ceremonies and Port Markers Project (MPCPMP). (2012, January 11). *Personal Stories of Captured Africans*. Retrieved from Middle Passage Ceremonies and Port Markers Project (MPCPMP): https://www.middlepassageproject.org/2012/01/11/personal-stories-of-captured-africans/.

[64] National Humanities Center. (2023, September 25). *Suicide among Slaves: A 'Very Last Resort.'* Retrieved from Nationalhumanitiesenter.org: https://nationalhumanitiescenter.org/pds/maai/emancipation/text2/suicide.pdf.

The psychological effects of the Atlantic slave trade on enslaved people were deep-seated and complex, often manifesting in various forms of mental disorders and a breakdown of basic human faculties like hope, trust, and the will to live. When we examine the psychological impacts closely, we expand our understanding of the slave trade and better appreciate the immense human suffering that is often overshadowed by the physical abuse that was inflicted upon the enslaved.

The 19th century saw the emergence of a new tomorrow for those held in bondage. Abolition stopped being a whimsical thought among intellectuals. Instead, it became a moving social force, and the possibility of emancipation for all slaves was openly discussed in general society.

Chapter 8: Abolition Movements: The Fight for Freedom and Equality

The abolitionist movement, which sought to dismantle the institution of slavery permanently, was one of the most influential social and political movements in the history of Western civilization. It did not happen overnight; it was a protracted struggle full of opposition and challenges. However, the ideological foundations that initially mobilized abolitionists were fundamentally rooted in moral imperatives, Enlightenment ideals, and theological convictions. Their discussions were much more than Sunday sermons.

Ideological Arguments

The intellectual ferment of the Enlightenment provided a fertile ground for the questioning of traditional institutions, including slavery. John Locke's concept of equality and Jean-Jacques Rousseau's explanation of the social contract provided intellectual and philosophical ammunition for the abolitionist cause, even if some of the key figures, such as John Locke, had complicated views or contracted their opinions on the institution.

Montesquieu used satire in his work, *The Spirit of the Laws*, to undermine the institution of slavery. He questioned the idea of natural slavery and exposed the arguments of pro-slavery advocates as being brutal, prideful, and absurd.[65]

Voltaire was another Enlightenment thinker who spoke up against the slave trade. His *Philosophical Dictionary* sharply criticized Europeans and the African kingdoms involved in the slave trade.

Adam Smith argued slavery was not only morally wrong but also economically inefficient. *Wealth of Nations* proposed that free labor was more productive and that slavery was a violation of free market principles.

Guillaume Thomas Raynal's *A Philosophical and Political History of the Settlements and Trade of the Europeans in the East and West Indies*, published in 1776, was a multi-volume work that is considered one of the primary texts of abolitionism in western Europe. Raynal did not attempt to spare anyone's feelings as he attacked the institution of slavery. In his book *Exile*, Raynal went to the heart of the matter in very strong words such as these:

"This insatiable thirst for gold has led to the most infamous, the most terrible of all trades, that of slaves. We're talking about crimes against nature, and it does not mention this one as the most execrable. Most nations of Europe are contaminated, and a keen interest stifled in their heart all feelings we owe to like."[66]

Enlightenment philosophers championed the power of reason and the value of the individual. Their application of rationalism and humanism on the question of slavery naturally led to questioning the moral and logical justifications for the slave trade.

Morality and Theology

Reason posed intellectual arguments against the institution of slavery. Moral arguments, however, were perhaps more straightforward and posited that the very institution was an affront to basic human dignity and ethical principles. Human beings have inherent worth and should not be treated as property to be sold, bought, or exploited. This argument drew on universal ethics espoused by religious and spiritual teachings.

---

[65] Schaub, D. (1990, Fall). *Race and the Constitution*. Retrieved from National Affairs: https://www.nationalaffairs.com/public_interest/detail/race-and-the-constitution.

[66] Experience France. (2023, September 30). *The Abbot Raynal, A True Inspiration to the French and American Revolutions*. Retrieved from Experiencemyfrance.com: https://experiencemyfrance.com/new-blog/the-abbot-raynal-a-true-inspiration-to-the-french-and-american-revolutions.

There were religious groups and denominations that took an active role in the abolitionist movement, some of which did so very early on. The Quakers were one of the earliest religious groups to doubt slavery, asserting that it was incompatible with Christian teachings about the equality and sanctity of all human beings.

John Wesley, the founder of the Methodist Church, wrote a pamphlet titled "Thoughts upon Slavery" in 1774 that served as a moral, religious indictment of the institution. Wesley pulled no punches with his attack on human bondage:

"Slavery imports an obligation of perpetual service, an obligation which only the consent of the master can dissolve. Neither in some countries can the master himself dissolve it, without the consent of Judges appointed by the law. It generally gives the master an arbitrary power of any correction, not affecting life or limb. Sometimes even these are exposed to his will, or protected only by a fine, or some slight punishment, too inconsiderable to restrain a master of a harsh temper. It creates an incapacity of acquiring anything, except for the master's benefit. It allows the master to alienate the same, in the same manner as his cows and horses. Lastly, it descends in its full extent from parent to child, even to the last generation."[67]

His pamphlet details the abuse and suffering that were all part of doing business in the Atlantic slave trade.

The Early Heroes

People did more than discuss the abuses of slavery in salons and coffee shops. Some were bold enough to go out into the open and publicly criticize the slave trade and those who were involved in it. They risked the anger and vengeance of some incredibly powerful people. It took courage to be an abolitionist.

Granville Sharp was an early champion for abolition, and he campaigned relentlessly to provide legal cases against the institution of slavery and create precedence for legal challenges. Olaudah Equiano, another abolitionist who was a former slave, gives a firsthand account of the horrors of the Middle Passage and slavery in his autobiography, *The Interesting Narrative of the Life of Olaudah Equiano*. William

---

[67] Msa.maryland.gov. (2023, September 30). *Thoughts upon Slavery*. Retrieved from Msa.maryland.gov:
https://msa.maryland.gov/megafile/msa/speccol/sc5300/sc5339/000091/000000/000001/restricted/2002_09_10/wesley/thoughtsuponslavery.html.

Wilberforce, a member of the British Parliament, began his quest to end slavery in the 18th century. He made sure that the high and mighty in British politics were made aware of the indignity and injustice of the Atlantic slave trade.

Eventually, the halls of the British Parliament were no longer a safe refuge for slave owners and their friends. Public opinion was demanding that the British government pay attention to what was going on in the colonies. The American and French Revolutions helped turn the spotlight on the ideas of freedom and fundamental human equality. The Atlantic slave trade was becoming unacceptable as an avenue for business.

Staring Down the Big Lie

The fight for freedom was an epic struggle. The pro-slavery faction included some of the wealthiest people in Great Britain and the United States. These people worked just as hard to maintain the status quo as the abolitionists did to end the Atlantic slave trade.

Slavery had been, without question, a significant contributor to profit derived from the New World. Plantation owners and traders didn't hesitate to argue that abolition would cripple economies that were reliant on slave-produced goods. Racial pseudoscience attempted to categorize races and portray Africans as naturally inferior and better suited for laborious tasks and second-class status. Religious justification, using selective biblical interpretations that were cherry-picked from the scriptures, was employed to argue that slavery was divinely ordained and that the Africans, the so-called descendants of Ham, were cursed to be servants and denied liberty because of sins committed in the far distant past.

The pro-slavery lobby in both the British Parliament and the United States Congress had considerable power, and they leveraged their wealth and connections to maintain the institution. The American pro-slavery bloc introduced the gag rule, which prohibited the debate on slavery in Congress. Several compromises, such as the Missouri Compromise and the Compromise of 1850, helped keep slavery alive.

The abolitionists used several means to fight back against these forces.

The Courts

An early abolitionist victory was the *Somerset v. Stewart* case. In 1772, William Murray, Lord Mansfield and chief justice of the court, ruled that a slave named James Somerset could not be transported forcibly out of England. Moreover, habeas corpus was a right available in England, even to slaves. It sent shockwaves through the British territories.[68]

Somerset's court victory proved that abolitionists could do more than spout platitudes on freedom or preach sermons. They could win before a judge and in the court of public opinion. Abolitionists would use the judicial system as often as possible to advance the cause of freedom.

- The *Zong* Decision (1783)

Some of these court cases shock us today because they give us a glimpse of the barbarity of the slave system. It was a given at the time that slaves were not really people but chattel property that could be bought, sold, and used. The *Zong* case is particularly frightening.

The *Zong* was a slave ship that took enslaved people on board in late 1781. Its captain, Luke Collingwood, was inexperienced and had never commanded a slave vessel before. He would oversee an atrocity on the ocean.

The *Zong* left the island of Saint Kitts with a hold full of slaves intended for the Jamaican market. The crew discovered the water barrels were leaking and that water supplies were getting low. A navigational mistake put the ship off course, and the *Zong* was becalmed off the southwest coast of Jamaica. It was nowhere near its destination of Kingston. Faced with the prospect of running out of water and the possibility of a slave insurrection, the captain and crew made a gruesome decision.

They decided to murder some of the slaves. On November 29th, 1781, fifty-four enslaved people were killed, and their bodies were thrown overboard. On December 1st, twenty-six more were killed and tossed overboard. Ten slaves committed suicide. The *Zong* finally reached port on December 22nd, 1781, and sold the rest of the enslaved still living. The ship was renamed the *Richard of Jamaica* and returned to England on October 26th, 1782. Events then became even more grotesque.

The Gregson syndicate owned the ship, and the owners filed an insurance claim to cover the loss of the murdered slaves at

---

[68] History and Collections. (2023, September 30). *The Somerset v Stewart Case*. Retrieved from English Heritage: https://www.english-heritage.org.uk/visit/places/kenwood/history-stories-kenwood/somerset-case/.

approximately £30 per victim. The claim was based on the insurance contract for the ship, which covered the deaths of slaves due to the perils of sailing the high seas. The insurance company disputed the claim, and the case went to the Court of King's Bench in London on May 22nd, 1783. The presiding judge, Lord Mansfield, made a horrific comment regarding this case:

"Had no doubt (though it shocks one very much) that the Case of Slaves was the same as if Horses had been thrown over board ... The Question was, whether there was not an Absolute Necessity for throwing them over board to save the rest? The Jury were of opinion there was."[69]

It was his belief that the insurance company had to pay for the dead slaves, "just as if Horses were kill'd" but that insurers did not have to pay for the slaves who died naturally, just as "you don't have to pay for horses that die a natural death."[70] The owners' request for financial relief was granted by the courts. They were awarded £3,660.

The verdict was appealed. A new trial was ordered, although it never took place. The owners ultimately did not receive a penny.

This all sounds terrible, but the modern reader has to understand the dynamics of risk management during the Atlantic slave trade. Slave traders routinely insured their cargo. If the boat simply sunk in a storm, the insurance claim for the value of the lost slaves in the storm would have been paid. The only restriction was that death had to arise from the perils of the sea. There would be no coverage for death through disease or insurrection. The West Indian slave trade is estimated to have accounted for almost 40 percent of the cargo insurance premium in the London insurance market of the late 18th century.

The owners might have won a case in a court of law, but they lost in the court of public opinion. Granville Sharp tried unsuccessfully to have the ship's crew prosecuted for murder. Nevertheless, the story of the massacre enraged the British public and boosted campaigns against slavery.[71]

---

[69] Burnard, T. (2023, September 30). *A New Look at the Zong Case of 1783*. Retrieved from OpenEdition Journals:
https://journals.openedition.org/1718/1808#:~:text=The%20murder%20of%20132%20African,history%20of%20eighteenth%2Dcentury%20abolitionism.

[70] Burnard, T. (2023, September 30). *A New Look at the Zong Case of 1783*.

[71] The Guardian. (2023, September 30). *The Story of the Zong Slave Ship: A Mass Murder Masquerading as an Insurance Claim*. Retrieved from theguardian.com:

- The *Amistad* Case (1841)

In February 1839, Portuguese slave hunters abducted Africans from present-day Sierra Leone (which was set up as a haven for former slaves) and shipped them to Cuba. The importation of enslaved people had been abolished by Spain, but that did not stop the illegal transatlantic slave trade. Havana was often the port of call for this unlawful commerce.

Fifty-three members of the abducted group were sold to Spanish plantation owners, and the slaves were placed on board a ship named the *Amistad* to voyage to Spanish plantations in Cuba.

A slave insurrection took place mid-journey in which the captain and the ship's cook were killed. The Africans ordered the remaining crew to take them back to Africa, but the crew changed course secretly at night. The *Amistad* instead sailed up the eastern coast of the United States. On August 26th, 1839, the ship was seized off the tip of Long Island.

The Africans were imprisoned under charges of murder and piracy, but those criminal charges were dropped. The court was left to define the legal status of these rebels and decide the property claims that were being made by the Spanish government and the plantation owners. Abolitionists raised money for the legal defense of the Africans, and the defense's argument was that these people had been illegally captured and imported as enslaved workers. The United States government wanted to send the Africans to Cuba to avoid trouble with Spain and argued against the kidnapped people.

The US District Court in Hartford ruled in January 1840 that the Africans were not Spanish slaves and should be returned to their homes. The decision was appealed to the Circuit Court, which upheld the district court's decision. A final appeal was made to the United States Supreme Court, which heard the case in early 1841.

Former President of the United States and current Congressman John Quincy Adams was brought in by the defense to plead the case of the enslaved people. Adams was a strong abolitionist and had been able to remove the gag rule that prohibited debate on slavery in Congress.

Adams was fierce in his defense. He declared the Africans had the right to fight for their freedom aboard the *Amistad* and invoked the

---

https://www.theguardian.com/law/2021/jan/19/the-story-of-the-zong-slave-ship-a-mass-masquerading-as-an-insurance-claim.

Declaration of Independence with these stirring words:

"The moment you come to the Declaration of Independence, that every man has a right to life and liberty, an inalienable right, this case is decided ... I ask nothing more in behalf of these unfortunate men, than this Declaration."

The Supreme Court ruled seven to one to uphold the lower courts' decisions. Abolitionists raised the money necessary to return the survivors to Africa.[72]

- Dred Scott (1857)

The final significant case in the abolitionist movement that we will look at took place in 1857. An enslaved man named Dred Scott sued for his freedom on the grounds that his residence in free territories should have made him free. The case went to the Supreme Court, and the decision was that slaves were non-citizens, meaning they could not sue the federal court. Furthermore, the Supreme Court declared Congress had no power to prohibit slavery in US territories.

This decision electrified the abolitionist movement and encouraged people to ignore the Fugitive Slave Act by helping slaves find their freedom in the North. The Underground Railroad, a network of abolitionist homes and farms where slaves found refuge while making their escape and finding a new home and life in the North, was a vital link in civil disobedience. Abolitionists who were involved risked the loss of property and imprisonment for ignoring the act. The Dred Scott decision was also one of the events that pushed the country toward the American Civil War.

These legal cases did more than just interpret the law. They shaped public sentiment, drove legislative agendas, and, in some instances, caused significant social upheavals. Efforts to drive the abolitionist movement into the background failed. Public sentiment continued to rise against slavery, and the media was instrumental in fanning the flames.

Media War against the Atlantic Slave Trade

The media in the late 18th and 19th centuries consisted of books, newspapers, and pamphlets. There was a strong effort to get the word out and to vote in candidates who would support the cause.

---

[72] History.com. (2023, June 27). *Amistad Case*. Retrieved from History.com: https://www.history.com/topics/slavery/amistad-case.

The Narratives of the Oppressed

Slavery advocates sought to dehumanize the victims of the Atlantic slave trade. To push back against this insidious disinformation, slave narratives were published. These were the accounts of former slaves who spoke openly about the abuses and the criminality of slavery in the Americas.

The slave narratives underscored the humanity, intellect, and emotions of enslaved people. Their detailed accounts of daily life, punishments, family separations, and physical and psychological torment gave others a look into the harsh realities of slavery that were often hidden or downplayed. Their experiences were plainly discussed.

These stories were frank discussions of the institution of slavery and how it affected society. The economic greed inherent in slavery was laid bare to the public. The narratives were also an emotional bridge that fostered empathy and inspired many to support abolition. There were many slave narratives, but a few stand out.

- *The Interesting Narrative of the Life of Olaudah Equiano* (1789)

Olaudah Equiano was a former slave who was kidnapped from his home in Africa and brought to the Americas. He eventually purchased his freedom and wrote the recollections of his life. His autobiography gives disturbing details of the Middle Passage and what slaves had to endure just to make it alive to the slave market. Olaudah Equiano's writing style is elegant, but the words he wrote describe a life of constant toil for people who didn't care whether a slave lived or died. If any reader had illusions about slavery when they opened the book, those fantasies were gone before the last chapter. Equiano painted the picture of a life devoid of hope and full of despair.

- *Narrative of the Life of Frederick Douglass, an American Slave* (1845)

Frederick Douglass was one of the greatest American orators of the mid-19th century. His eloquence could hold a crowd spellbound, and his message was powerful. The writings of Douglass were equally mesmerizing. His autobiography told the story of his life in bondage. The book also challenged American society. He criticized its views on justice and the distribution of slavery. The publication of the book was a watershed moment for the abolitionist movement.

- *Incidents in the Life of a Slave Girl* (1861)

   Harriet Jacobs, using the pseudonym Linda Brent, wrote a narrative that spoke of the specific hardships and sexual exploitation faced by women in slavery. Her account of the struggles for freedom, especially for her children, provided a perspective that was missing from the male narratives.

   These narratives were more than mere autobiographical accounts. They were calls for reform and challenged society on both sides of the Atlantic by confronting the grim realities of the Atlantic slave trade. By giving voice to the voiceless, slave narratives were able to rally public opinion against slavery.

The Power of the Press

The 19th century saw a surge in literacy, with newspapers playing a pivotal role in shaping public opinion and discourse. The press amplified the voice of the enslaved, reported on anti-slavery activities, and served as the nexus for abolitionist thought. Several newspapers stood out from the rest.

- *The Liberator* (1831-1865)

   William Lloyd Garrison was the editor of *The Liberator*, and he risked his life to get the abolitionist story to the public. His unwavering stance on the immediate emancipation of slaves was the tone of the newspaper. Garrison's editorials argued against slavery and called for radical action.

- *The North Star* (1847-1851)

   This newspaper was the creation of Frederick Douglass. It was named after the guiding star that led runaway slaves north. Douglass used this publication as a platform for his oratory and writings. *The North Star* went beyond emancipation. It was also a champion for women's rights and other social reforms.

- *The National Anti-Slavery Standard* (1840-1870)

   The *National Anti-Slavery Standard* was the official newspaper of the American Anti-Slavery Society and reached a wide audience. Throughout its life, this newspaper chronicled the abolitionist movement's major events, including the American Civil War, and gave a steady voice to abolitionism.

The pages of these newspapers brought to light the brutal realities of slavery, challenged social norms, and forged a sense of community among abolitionists. Media were weapons of justice, leading to significant legislation that ended slavery.

Freedom Legislation

It was a gradual process, but the abolitionist movement moved from the media and courts to the governing bodies of Great Britain and the United States. The ultimate legislative success was the result of the tireless efforts of champions who refused to be shouted down, ridiculed, or threatened.

William Wilberforce was a power for freedom in the British Parliament. He advocated for the abolition of slavery long before it was fashionable to do so.

The Slave Trade Act of 1807

Despite abolition bills routinely failing, the abolitionist movement was undeterred. A petition campaign set the stage for the Foreign Slave Trade Abolition Bill of 1806. The bill was intended to prevent British traders from importing slaves into territories belonging to foreign countries. Wilberforce and his allies in Parliament made very few comments about it as a maneuver to get the bill passed by its opponents, and the bill was introduced to Parliament on January 2nd, 1807, in the House of Lords. It was championed by British Prime Minister Lord Grenville.

The bill went to the House of Commons on February 10th, 1807, and passed by a vote of 283 to 16. The Slave Trade Act received royal assent on March 25th, 1807. The British slave trade involving the West Indies, the Americas, and West Africa was formally abolished. After years of advocating for what some people believed to be a lost cause, William Wilberforce won his victory and received a standing ovation.[73]

The United States followed suit on January 1st, 1808. Federal legislation made it illegal to bring captured people into the United States from Africa, although there were still instances where slaves were brought into the United States.

Even though the transatlantic shipment of slaves was prohibited, it did not mean that the institution ended. The British had to clear one more

---

[73] UK Parliament. (2023, September 30). *Parliament Abolishes the Slave Trade*. Retrieved from Parliament.uk: https://www.parliament.uk/about/living-heritage/transformingsociety/tradeindustry/slavetrade/overview/parliament-abolishes-the-slave-trade/.

hurdle.

Slave Abolition Act of 1833

Slave revolts in Jamaica helped spur the final action to eradicate slavery in the British Empire. The Slave Abolition Act of 1833 received royal assent on August 28th, 1833. The act had two major parts.

1. The emancipation of all slaves throughout the British Empire, except those territories held by the British East India Company: Ceylon and Saint Helena.
2. Slave owners were compensated for the loss of their slaves. The government took out loans to pay for the compensation.

The impact was that 800,000 African slaves in the Caribbean, Canada, and Africa were freed. Great Britain's role as a slave trader and a slave owner was officially over.[74] Wilberforce died three days after he was told that the Slave Abolition Act of 1833 was passed by Parliament.

The United States took longer to adopt legislation to end bondage, but the country eventually put laws in place that ended the institution.

Northwest Ordinance of 1787

The Northwest Ordinance was the first effort by the new nation to end slavery. It was not legislation, but it prohibited slavery in the Northwest Territory and created a precedent for limiting slavery's expansion.

It was not so much the existence of slavery but rather its expansion in the United States that caused considerable turmoil. In the first half of the 19th century, slavery in the South was an ingrained institution, but many people in the North did not want slavery to continue to expand across the nation. If there were more slave states than free states, the balance of power would quickly get out of hand.

America put in place a series of compromises, which did not solve the problem. Legislation like the Fugitive Slave Act only made things worse. In the end, the only way to decide the matter was through aggression. The American Civil War began in 1861, which led to significant action regarding slavery.

---

[74] The History Press. (2023, September 30). *The Slavery Abolition Act of 1833*. Retrieved from Thehistorypress.co.uk: https://www.thehistorypress.co.uk/articles/the-slavery-abolition-act-of-1833/.

The Emancipation Proclamation (1863)

It has been argued that Abraham Lincoln cared more about preserving the Union than breaking the bonds holding enslaved people. Lincoln proved to be an astute politician and waited for an opportunity, a Union victory, to advance the freedom of those held in bondage.

The Emancipation Proclamation, issued on January 1st, 1863, declared the freedom of slaves held in Confederate territory. It did nothing for slaves held in the border states. Regardless, the Emancipation Proclamation made abolition government policy and showed that the war would result in the freedom of the enslaved. Its issuance also convinced Great Britain not to give significant aid to the Confederacy.

The Thirteenth Amendment (1865)

The movie *Lincoln* tells the story of how Abraham Lincoln maneuvered to secure the passage of the Thirteenth Amendment. This was a masterpiece of lobbying, and it demonstrates the political skills of America's sixteenth president.

The Thirteenth Amendment was the formal and legal end of slavery in the United States. It freed millions and altered the social fabric of the United States for the better. Reconstruction, which followed the Civil War, led to some heinous decisions, such as the Jim Crow laws, the impact of which can still be felt to this day.

In Summary

There were some holdouts, but the tide had turned irrevocably against enslaving people. Denmark was the first to end the slave trade, passing a law in 1792 that decreed its end in 1803. Haiti was the first Western country to end the institution of slavery, doing so at the moment of its conception in 1804. Slavery in Cuba was abolished in 1886. The final country in the Western Hemisphere to end slavery, Brazil, did so on May 13th, 1888.

After hundreds of years of promoting oppression and abuse, the Atlantic slave trade was officially over.

Chapter 9: The Legacy of the Atlantic Slave Trade

The Atlantic slave trade was a grim business that created the African diaspora and redrew demographic, cultural, and economic contours across continents. It did not exist in a vacuum; the enduring legacies of this trade are cultural and economic and can still be felt today.

The Concept of Race

The significance of a person's skin color did not always have the same connotations as it does today. Africans of color were found in medieval Europe, and negative comments were not commonly made about their appearance. The Atlantic slave trade changed that neutral opinion when the demand for forced labor in the Americas grew. There were fewer indigenous people to force into servitude, and the use of indentured white servants became less attractive. Black Africans became desired as a forced labor pool. People used the color of a person's skin and race, as well as cultural and societal norms, to justify this reasoning. For most, it became natural to assume that Africans were naturally inferior.[75] Unfortunately, that concept continues to be prevalent among some circles even today.

---

[75] Pbs.org. (2023, September 30). *Race: The Power of an Illusion.* Retrieved from Pbs.org: https://www.pbs.org/race/000_About/002_04-background-02-03.htm.

Inferiority in West Africa

The Atlantic slave trade caused human beings to be considered commodities, products that could be bought and sold. Slavery did exist in West Africa before the Europeans, but in many places, it was more of a form of indentured servitude. The international slave trade fostered an environment where leaders could become even more wealthy by attacking their neighbors and securing prisoners of war for future sale.

There were states in West Africa that specialized in the slave trade, and there were regions in the interior where raids were conducted. This has caused tensions in modern African states. People remember those who were slave merchants. There are West African communities where members are prohibited from marrying anyone who is descended from a slave merchant.

Benin is a country where the present is still haunted by the past. There are internal divisions that have their roots in slave commerce. In the 2016 presidential election, a candidate pointed out in a televised debate that his opponent was a descendant of slave merchants. For some nations, it's almost impossible to eradicate memories of the slave trade.[76]

Creole Hierarchies

Intermingling between blacks and whites in the Americas could not be avoided. From these associations, the Creole social class arose. Some Creoles could identify as black or white. A Creole could be light-skinned color, brown-skinned, or dark-skinned and might enjoy a certain degree of privilege due to their perceived whiteness. Creolization has led to distinct cultural identities that pit pure African identities against Creole identities.[77]

Culture

Twelve to twenty million Africans were forced to leave their homes, which created demographic imbalances that exacerbated the sociopolitical environment in West Africa. The diaspora took people away from their cultures and forced them to establish a new cultural

---

[76] Sief, K. (2018, January 29). *An African Country Reckons with Its History of Selling Slaves*. Retrieved from Washington Post.com: https://www.washingtonpost.com/world/africa/an-african-country-reckons-with-its-history-of-selling-slaves/2018/01/29/5234f5aa-ff9a-11e7-86b9-8908743c79dd_story.html.

[77] Wiltz, A. (2023, April 19). *Are Creole People a Privileged or Oppressed, or Somewhere in Between?* Retrieved from Medium.com: https://medium.com/louisiana-creoles/are-creole-people-a-privileged-or-oppressed-or-somewhere-in-between-2f352a9882e.

identity of their own in the New World.

Some examples include the samba and the bossa nova in Brazil, which intertwine African rhythm and dance. Afro-Cuban jazz and son cubano are staples of Cuban culture, which embody African rhythmic patterns woven into European musical elements. The rumba and salsa are both rooted in African dance traditions. Reggae and calypso in the West Indies display African musical traditions as well.

Religion has also been influenced by West African ties. Candomblé and Umbanda epitomize African spiritual beliefs that have been intermingled with Catholic and indigenous spirituality. Cuban Santería and Haitian Vodou are also examples of African religious beliefs that were mixed with Catholicism and indigenous beliefs. The beliefs and customs of West Africa were not left on the slave ships; they traveled to the Americas and intermingled with already existing beliefs and ideas.

The cultural panorama of the Caribbean, in particular, has profound African influences. It is a living legacy that not only attests to a historical narrative of endurance and creativity in the face of slavery but also contributes significantly to the global dialog. There is a vibrant cultural tapestry in the Americas that continues to reverberate.

Sadly, there are still traces of the Atlantic slave trade in current society. Granted, all of the players in the Atlantic slave trade are dead, but some of its legacies endure. There is a need for mending and healing to allow societies on both sides of the Atlantic to thrive in the future.

The Question of Reparations

The topic of reparations has been discussed in the last few years as a means of correcting the injustices committed years ago. Reparations are often discussed in terms of sums of money to be paid to the descendants of enslaved people. This is a divisive topic that has garnered strong opinions on both sides. Nevertheless, there are ways that changes and reforms can bring closure to a horrendous period in world history. We are going to talk about a few to get an idea of what has been discussed in the past.

Put an End to Obroni W'awu

Obroni w'awu is an Akan phrase that means "dead white man's clothes." The secondhand clothes usually found in Goodwill stores are exported to Ghana, where they are sold in the Kantamanto market. Ghana is one of the biggest secondhand clothing markets in the world, and most of this merchandise comes from Great Britain.

The problem Ghana faces is that nearly 40 percent of the used clothing rots in landfills. Approximately fifty tons a day are discarded, and they are sometimes dumped on the beaches, creating an enormous environmental problem. The primary culprits are major players in the fast fashion industry. Ghana has become a country of choice for the waste management industry.

The consequences are damaging not only the environment but also the textile industries of West Africa. Simple solutions include a ban on the export of clothing that has synthetic material and a return of containers filled with low-value textiles. These restrictions can stop Ghana from becoming a dumping ground.

The fashion industry can also help. Companies could build clothing factories in West Africa for ready-to-wear clothing and shoes. If these companies can use Bangladesh as an apparel manufacturing center, they can easily build factories in Accra or Porto-Novo.[78]

Renegotiate the Economic Partnership Agreements

The European Union (EU) is Africa's largest trading partner. Countries in the EU have used tariffs and agricultural subsidies to make European products cheaper than African imports, limiting the chance for African countries to have access to European markets. Economic Partnership Agreements (EPAs) give Europe access to African markets. However, subsidized

European exports, such as milk, depreciate prices and undermine African domestic competitors. The EPAs can be renegotiated so that European prices charged to African consumers are not artificially lower due to subsidies.[79]

Return What Was Stolen

Artwork is a significant part of a country's cultural heritage, and important pieces of art were looted from West Africa during the Scramble of Africa, a period of time when European nations rushed to secure their African territories. A primary example is the Benin Bronzes. These were looted from Benin City in modern-day Nigeria by British

---

[78] Davies, B. (2020, February 25). *The Fast Fashion Trash Mountain.* Retrieved from Dailymail.co.uk: https://www.dailymail.co.uk/news/article-8044313/Shocking-report-reveals-cheap-clothes-resold-end-rotting-Africa.html.
[79] Buhari, M. (2022, February 17). *It's Time for a New Economic Deal between the EU and Africa.* Retrieved from Politico.com: https://www.politico.eu/article/its-time-for-a-new-economic-deal-between-the-eu-and-africa/.

soldiers who plundered the city. These sculptures reside in the British Museum today.

Several museums, including the Smithsonian Institution and the Metropolitan Museum of Art, decided to return art that was stolen over one hundred years ago. The act is commendable, but many people believe there is more to be done.

There are still African works of art taken during colonial times that remain in European museums and universities. Many people believe they need to be returned to their place of origin. It could cause other works of art to be returned to their homes, such as the Elgin Marbles being sent back to Greece and various paintings that were stolen from Catholic cathedrals and universities sent back to where they came from.[80]

End of the CFA Franc

Several West African nations, including those that had been affected by the slave trade, rely on the CFA franc as their currency. The arrangement requires a percentage of the participating countries' assets to be held in French banks.

A challenge for this relationship is that it hinders the competitiveness of African products by acting as a tax on exports and a subsidy for imports. Moreover, financing is more expensive, and interest rates for loans are exceptionally high.

In many people's minds, the CFA franc has outlived its usefulness. A new currency, the eco, would encourage new investors and solve some problems African countries are experiencing with the old currency.[81]

Mobile Phones

Mobile phones are more than a means of connecting to friends in West Africa. Ownership of cell phones is very high in sub-Saharan Africa, and mobile phones have a positive impact on education, the economy, and communication. People in Western Europe and the United States are urged not to dispose of their mobile phones but to donate them to Africa.

---

[80] Mohin, A. (2023, June 5). *Who Owns the Benin Bronzes? The Answer Just Got More Complicated.* Retrieved from NYTimes.com: https://www.nytimes.com/2023/06/04/arts/design/benin-bronzes-nigeria-ownership.html .
[81] Societe Generale. (2022, June 12). *From The CFA Franc To The eco, A Reform for the Convergence of West African Economies.* Retrieved from Societegenerale.com.

Mobile phone companies such as T-Mobile and Apple could do more to eradicate the final vestiges of the Atlantic slave trade by giving their products to people in West Africa for free. This would further stimulate the use of social media and help small businesses in countries that sorely need assistance.

Those companies could go one step further by constructing manufacturing centers to produce mobile phones and spare parts. Local consumers will provide the demand to make the operations profitable.[82]

Other initiatives such as microloans and supporting the creation of historical education centers, such as the one being developed in Barbados, are also ways to bring an end to what is left of the Atlantic slave trade.

The United States

Although the Atlantic slave trade sent less than one million enslaved people to what is now the United States, problems remain from slavery and the Jim Crow era. Political science experts believe some changes can be made to promote a better sense of social justice. The legal system is where some significant reforms can be introduced.

Sentencing

Fredrik DeBoer is an American professor who has written on social justice issues in America. In his recent book, *How Elites Ate the Social Justice Movement*, DeBoer noted the rate of imprisonment for blacks was 1,1240 per 100,000 in 2021, which is significantly higher than the 261 per 100,000 for white Americans. Criminal conviction caused 6.2 percent of adult African Americans to be disenfranchised in the 2020 election as opposed to 1.7 percent of the non-black population.[83]

Sentencing is a complex issue. It is crucial to make sure that minorities are represented on juries, but a hard look at sentencing is necessary. Sentences for various crimes are not cast in stone. Crimes that were once felonies can be reexamined in the light of changing times and reduced to misdemeanors. For some criminals, longer probationary periods may be better than time spent incarcerated in prisons.

---

[82] Johnson, L. S. (2018, October 9). *Majorities in Sub-Saharan Africa Own Mobile Phones, But Smartphone Adoption Is Modest*. Retrieved from Pew Research Center: https://www.pewresearch.org/global/2018/10/09/majorities-in-sub-saharan-africa-own-mobile-phones-but-smartphone-adoption-is-modest/.

[83] DeBoer, F. (2023). *How Elites Ate The Social Justice Movement*. New York, NY: Simon & Schuster.

Incarceration is made longer by multiple sentences. For example, a person who robs a store and then flees in a car with expired license plates and an expired driver's license can face sentences for the robbery and for various auto-related infractions. The sentences can add years to a person's time in prison. An alternative would be a term of imprisonment no more than what the most severe crime committed allows, which cuts down on the time spent in jail and the taxes used to house and feed that person. It also allows the person to return to society sooner.

Expungement is the means by which a person's criminal record is wiped clean after a period of time. An individual whose criminal record has been expunged can apply for a job knowing that past infractions will not stop them from obtaining meaningful employment. Felonies may be excluded from expungement because of the seriousness of the crime, but expungement of misdemeanors could be made much easier and less expensive.

Education

Project Baltimore recently reported that twenty-three schools in Baltimore, Maryland, did not have a single student doing math at grade level according to standardized tests. Only 7 percent of third through eighth graders in Baltimore's public schools tested proficient in math.

Education is critical in a knowledge-driven economy. Those figures suggest that no matter what efforts are made to improve employment, minority job applicants are doomed to failure. It takes more than larger school budgets to change that.[84]

Many corporations brag about their diversity awareness initiatives. That is terrific, but some wonder if it would be better if those same companies invested in reading and math programs in the inner city where many minorities live. Encouraging employees to become reading or math tutors would go a long way in guaranteeing that those students will be successful later in life.

Focus on Employment Figures

Social justice activists point to data from the Bureau of Labor Statistics to demonstrate employment inequities. That is fine, but there is a better source of information.

---

[84] Papst, C. (2023, September 18). *At 13 Baltimore City High Schools, Zero Students Tested Proficient on 2023 State Math Exam*. Retrieved from Foxbaltimore.com:
https://foxbaltimore.com/news/project-baltimore/at-13-baltimore-city-high-schools-zero-students-tested-proficient-on-2023-state-math-exam.

Private sector employers with one hundred or more employees and federal contractors with fifty or more employees must submit workforce demographic data, including data by job category and sex and race or ethnicity, to the Equal Employment Opportunity Commission (EEOC). Combined with affirmative action information, the data can assess whether an employer has made a good faith effort to remove unlawful barriers to employment, increase employment opportunities, and produce measurable results. Good faith efforts can include apprenticeship programs, tuition reimbursement, effective job postings, and recruitment efforts that are intended to hire underrepresented minorities. Taking a look at the EEOC and affirmative action data presents a better picture of the efforts made to end discriminatory hiring practices that were once commonplace in the US.[85]

The above are just suggested ways of providing some relief to those still affected by the consequences of the Atlantic slave trade. There are other possibilities that should also be explored.

---

[85] US Equal Employment Opportunity Commission. (2023, September 30). *EEO-1 Data Collection*. Retrieved from Eeoc.gov: https://www.eeoc.gov/data/eeo-1-data-collection#:~:text=The%20EEO%2D1%20Component%201,race%20or%20ethnicity%2C%20to%20the.

Chapter 10: Reexamining History: Critical Perspectives on the Slave Trade

History is a textbook for the human race. The study of the past allows us to review how different people dealt with events or changes that dramatically affected their lives and that of their children. What history cannot be is a collection of fables.

The Atlantic slave trade generated copious amounts of texts on the businesses and economies that were centered on human beings as a commodity. We should be shocked at some of the stories that came out of the Middle Passage. However, we must be sure that these are not unsubstantiated legends woven from thin air. The facts must supersede our emotions.

The Narratives

Slave narratives are an important source of information about the Atlantic slave trade. In them, we have the personal accounts of those who endured the voyage and the humiliation of the auction block. The original intent was to inform the public of the horrors of enslavement. However, the text was also meant to shock the reader into taking action and talking about abolition. The narratives were a direct appeal to a person's conscience.

The authenticity of the slave narratives deserves some form of assessment for accuracy. Comparing two narratives that were written at separate times can help. For instance, the work of Olaudah Equiano can be compared with the story of another slave who endured the transatlantic crossing, Joseph Cinque, the leader of the *Amistad* rebellion.

Commonly held stereotypes can be challenged in the narratives. We often think of slave owners as evil psychopaths. Yet, in Solomon Northrop's *Twelve Years a Slave*, the slaveholder William Ford is portrayed as a kind and religious man. However, this does not mean that slavery was a benign institution. Instead, an irony emerges that juxtaposes Ford's Christian values with the dehumanizing institution in which he was an active participant. Righteous slaveholders were wrapped in the chains of hypocrisy forged by an institution that made them rich but contradicted their values.

Essential Databases

Databases emerged as crucial messengers from the past, carrying information encapsulated in statistics. They help give us an understanding of the enormity of the Atlantic slave trade and its impact on transcontinental commerce. The databases also serve as a source of healing. Many people of African descent complain that they do not know where they came from or the history of the customs they practice. The databases clarify things.

An example of an excellent database of the Atlantic slave trade is the Trans-Atlantic Slave Trade Database. This holds information about over thirty-six thousand voyages between the 16th and the 19th centuries. It is a treasure trove of primary data that includes information about slave ships, their point of origin, their destination, and the enslaved individuals trapped below decks.

Seminal Research: African Founders

Pulitzer Prize winner David Hackett Fischer released a major work on slavery, *African Founders: How Enslaved People Expanded American Ideals*, in 2022. The work is the result of years of research and is significant historiography for several reasons.

It tells the story of slavery in the thirteen British colonies of North America. A reader can take a look at the various laws governing slavery in colonies like Pennsylvania and Massachusetts, as well as the southern colonies. The author does not pull any punches. He describes a slave cemetery found in New York City where human remains show evidence of backbreaking work. He also writes about laws in various colonies that gave enslaved people specific rights in courts.

The most valuable information that Fischer shares is the skill-based enslavement that was a part of the Atlantic slave trade. Slave traders were not just looking for bodies; they also wanted skilled workers. The book tells of how individuals were often chosen based on their expertise. Slaveholders in the Americas were looking for individuals adept in agriculture, metallurgy, or other crafts. The slave trade targeted regions in Africa known for various skills as a result. Areas where the people were known to be rebellious were often ignored.

Fischer's discussion of skills-based enslavement permits researchers and readers alike to understand that the Atlantic slave trade developed into a very sophisticated economic sector based on forced labor.

Analyzing History

History is sometimes used to justify a preconceived notion or theory. This means the historical conclusion is stated and then facts are gathered to support it rather than the other way around. That's a dangerous way of looking at the historical record and has resulted in pseudo-history being published and disseminated as the truth.

A textbook example of this is the Lost Cause. This view of history argues that slavery was not the leading cause of the American Civil War and that the Confederacy was a noble undertaking. There were other issues that led to the Civil War, but when you dig at those issues, slavery is at the root of all of them. The Lost Cause is a myth-based view of the historical record that, unfortunately, made its way into the books of American public schools. It has taken decades to remove this lie from the pages. Thus, it is essential we examine the past without wearing ideological blinders.

Interpretive history is an important means of analyzing the past. Essentially, interpretive history looks at a period of time as a static picture. The historian or researcher looks at primary (firsthand) and secondary (scholarly) historical sources and derives an explanation based on the interpretation of the facts. It is possible that there may be more than one explanation, given the individual evaluating the events. What is significant is that any interpretation is based on facts and not politics or emotions.

Interpretation of the facts can be embarrassing. Hannah Arendt walked into a firestorm of criticism and anger when her book, *Eichmann in Jerusalem*, accused Jewish leaders of collaborating with the Nazis.[86] The same can be said for interpretive analysis of slavery and the Atlantic slave trade. There is no doubt that the collaboration of various African rulers made it easy to fulfill the demand for slaves, and slave raids into the interior were seen as sources of revenue.

Some cherished beliefs can also be called into question. The story of Crispus Attucks and the Boston Massacre is often used to show the participation of blacks in the fight for American freedom from the British Crown. Yet, Simon Schama's book *Rough Crossings* notes that many blacks in the South were Tories and fought against the Continental Army.[87]

Interpretive history goes beyond reciting dates and events to an analysis and interpretation of events and ideas. The past is taken into context, and presentism is not permitted to distort the historical picture. The reward is an analysis that comes closer to the truth.

That is an essential point when it comes to examining history. It happens too often that social activists of one type or another will seek to get their agenda written into the pages of the past. This political posturing often hides the facts from the public. Presentism holds the danger of introducing too many modern notions that do not give an accurate picture of the motivations and situations that caused people to do what they did.

The Atlantic slave trade cannot be dismissed as a minor historical occurrence. It created and destroyed economies and changed cultures on both sides of the Atlantic. The analysis of the Atlantic slave trade has one firm conclusion: slavery is wrong, and forced labor is not an acceptable means of getting the job done.

---

[86] Robin, C. (2015, May 12). *The Trials of Hannah Arendt.* Retrieved from The Nation: https://www.thenation.com/article/archive/trials-hannah-arendt/.
[87] Schama, S. (2006). *Rough Crossings.* New York, NY: HarperCollins Publishers.

Conclusion

The Atlantic slave trade is a tale of human tendency to be inhumane. There is very little redeeming about what took place, and it was the heroic struggles of enslaved people and abolitionists who finally convinced public opinion that slavery was innately evil. A regrettable consequence of the saga is that it confirms that human beings are not always as kind and compassionate as we would want them to be. Avarice can turn even the best souls into devils.

Nevertheless, the story must be told. We have to keep in mind that just as people are capable of doing beautiful things, there is a base part of human nature that encourages them to put profit over decency. Greed was the driving force behind what happened in the Middle Passage.

The historiography of the Atlantic slave trade has progressed over the years. We do not have to rely solely on narratives anymore. There are many databases that allow us to analyze what happened. Some figures are disturbing, but accurate data paints a picture that is not tainted by legends or deliberate distortions. However, it is important to remember that these figures and statistics were actual humans who suffered.

Studying the Atlantic slave trade allows us to better understand certain cultural norms present in West Africa. There are tensions in West Africa that can be traced to the slave trade, including some groups hating others because of the role the latter played in facilitating enslavement. Discovering the original reasons for lingering animosities will hopefully help create resolutions and promote healing.

Without question, the Atlantic slave trade was a terrifying and horrific episode in human history. It is also a reflection on the tenacity of those who, although cramped below deck in the holds of slave vessels, refused to part with their cultural heritage. They took their values with them and had the courage to maintain them in the face of suppression.

If you enjoyed this book, a review on Amazon would be greatly appreciated because it would mean a lot to hear from you.

To leave a review:
1. Open your camera app.
2. Point your mobile device at the QR code.
3. The review page will appear in your web browser.

Thanks for your support!

Here's another book by Enthralling History that you might like

Free limited time bonus

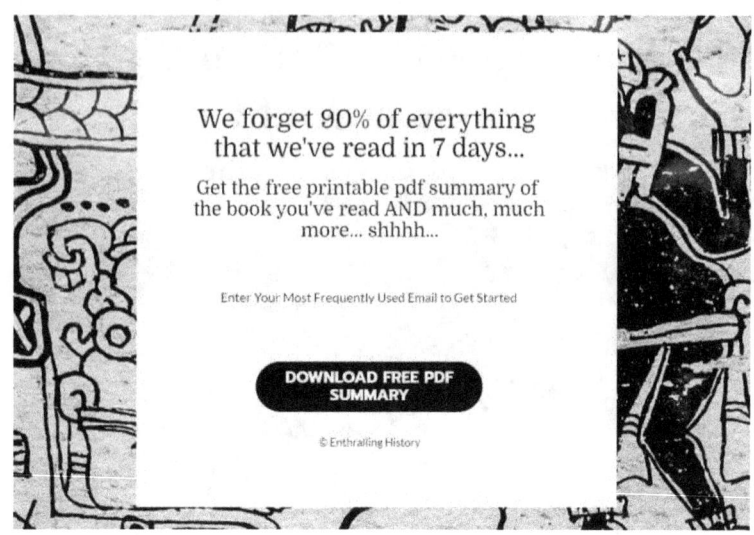

Stop for a moment. We have a free bonus set up for you. The problem is this: we forget 90% of everything that we read after 7 days. Crazy fact, right? Here's the solution: we've created a printable, 1-page pdf summary for this book that you're reading now. All you have to do to get your free pdf summary is to go to the following website: https://livetolearn.lpages.co/enthrallinghistory/

Or, Scan the QR code!

Once you do, it will be intuitive. Enjoy, and thank you!

Bibliography

Abdul Mohamud, R. W. (2018, June 21). *Britain's Involvement with the New World: Slavery and the Transatlantic Slave Trade.* Retrieved from Bl.uk: https://www.bl.uk/restoration-18th-century-literature/articles/britains-involvement-with-new-world-slavery-and-the-transatlantic-slave-trade.

African Passages, Lowcountry Adaptions. (2023, September 25). *Slavery before the Trans-Atlantic Trade.* Retrieved from African Passages, Lowcountry Adaptions: HYPERLINK "https://ldhi.library.cofc.edu/exhibits/show/africanpassageslowcountryadapt/introductionatlanticworld/slaverybeforetrade" https://ldhi.library.cofc.edu/exhibits/show/africanpassageslowcountryadapt/introductionatlanticworld/slaverybeforetrade .

Arantes, J. T. (2021, July 14). *Study Highlights the Role of Diplomatic Relations between Dahomey and Brazil in the Slave Trade.* Retrieved from Agencia FAPESP: HYPERLINK "https://agencia.fapesp.br/study-highlights-the-role-of-diplomatic-relations-between-dahomey-and-brazil-in-the-slave-trade/36328" https://agencia.fapesp.br/study-highlights-the-role-of-diplomatic-relations-between-dahomey-and-brazil-in-the-slave-trade/36328 .

Araujo, A. L. (2022, September 16). *The Woman King Softens the Truth of the Slave Trade.* Retrieved from Slate.com: https://slate.com/culture/2022/09/woman-king-movie-true-story-dahomey-amazons-slave-trade.html.

Bibb, H. Chapter IX. https://pressbooks.library.torontomu.ca/henrybibb/chapter/9/.

Bradshaw, J. (2023, October 1). *Saint-Domingue Revolution.* Retrieved from 64 Parishes: HYPERLINK "https://64parishes.org/entry/saint-domingue-revolution?gclid=EAIaIQobChMIztKE2JqtgQMVRA6zAB1uKgxcEAAYAiA

AEgL9sPD_BwE." https://64parishes.org/entry/saint-domingue-revolution?gclid=EAIaIQobChMIztKE2JqtgQMVRA6zAB1uKgxcEAAYAiA AEgL9sPD_BwE.

Britannica.com. (2023, October 1). *Haitian Revolution.* Retrieved from Britannica.com: HYPERLINK "https://www.britannica.com/topic/Haitian-Revolution%20" https://www.britannica.com/topic/Haitian-Revolution

Britannica.com. (2023, September 19). *Sugarcane and the Growth of Slavery.* Retrieved from Britannica.com: HYPERLINK "https://www.britannica.com/place/Cuba/Sugarcane-and-the-growth-of-slavery." https://www.britannica.com/place/Cuba/Sugarcane-and-the-growth-of-slavery.

Brown, William. *Narrative of William W. Brown.* HYPERLINK "https://docsouth.unc.edu/neh/brown47/brown47.html" https://docsouth.unc.edu/neh/brown47/brown47.html .

Buhari, M. (2022, February 17). *It's Time for a New Economic Deal between the EU and Africa.* Retrieved from Politico.com: HYPERLINK "https://www.politico.eu/article/its-time-for-a-new-economic-deal-between-the-eu-and-africa/" https://www.politico.eu/article/its-time-for-a-new-economic-deal-between-the-eu-and-africa/ .

Burnard, T. (2023, September 30). *A New Look at the Zong Case of 1783.* Retrieved from OpenEdition Journals: https://journals.openedition.org/1718/1808#:~:text=The%20murder%20of%20 132%20African,history%20of%20eighteenth%2Dcentury%20abolitionism.

Charleston County Public Library. (2023, Septermber 18). *Nearly 1,000 Cargos: The Legacy of Importing Africans into Charleston.* Retrieved from Charleston County Public Library: HYPERLINK "https://www.ccpl.org/charleston-time-machine/nearly-1000-cargos-legacy-importing-africans-charleston" https://www.ccpl.org/charleston-time-machine/nearly-1000-cargos-legacy-importing-africans-charleston .

Charleston SC. (2023, September 19). *Old Slave Mart Museum.* Retrieved from Chaleston-sc.gov: HYPERLINK "https://www.charleston-sc.gov/160/Old-Slave-Mart-Museum" https://www.charleston-sc.gov/160/Old-Slave-Mart-Museum .

Choi, M. (2023, September 25). *Necessary Violence in Frederick Douglass's Narrative.* Retrieved from Methodist.edu: HYPERLINK "https://www.methodist.edu/wp-content/uploads/2022/06/mr2020_choi.pdf" https://www.methodist.edu/wp-content/uploads/2022/06/mr2020_choi.pdf .

Davies, B. (2020, February 25). *The Fast Fashion Trash Mountain.* Retrieved from Dailymail.co.uk: HYPERLINK "https://www.dailymail.co.uk/news/article-8044313/Shocking-report-reveals-cheap-clothes-resold-end-rotting-Africa.html" https://www.dailymail.co.uk/news/article-8044313/Shocking-report-reveals-cheap-clothes-resold-end-rotting-Africa.html .

DeBoer, F. (2023). *How Elites Ate The Social Justice Movement.* New York, NY: Simon & Schuster.

Experience France. (2023, September 30). *The Abbot Raynal, A True Inspiration to the French and American Revolutions.* Retrieved from Experiencemyfrance.com: HYPERLINK "https://experiencemyfrance.com/new-blog/the-abbot-raynal-a-true-inspiration-to-the-french-and-american-revolutions" https://experiencemyfrance.com/new-blog/the-abbot-raynal-a-true-inspiration-to-the-french-and-american-revolutions .

Henson, J. *Truth Stanger than Fiction.* HYPERLINK "https://docsouth.unc.edu/neh/henson58/henson58.html" https://docsouth.unc.edu/neh/henson58/henson58.html .

Historical Society of Pennsylvania. (2008, September 11). *An English Slave Trader, an African Prince & the Pennsylvania Gazette.* Retrieved from Historical Society of Pennsylvania: HYPERLINK "https://hsp.org/blogs/hidden-histories/an-english-slave-trader-an-african-prince-the-pennsylvania-gazette" https://hsp.org/blogs/hidden-histories/an-english-slave-trader-an-african-prince-the-pennsylvania-gazette .

History and Collections. (2023, September 30). *The Somerset v Stewart Case.* Retrieved from English Heritage: HYPERLINK "https://www.english-heritage.org.uk/visit/places/kenwood/history-stories-kenwood/somerset-case/" https://www.english-heritage.org.uk/visit/places/kenwood/history-stories-kenwood/somerset-case/ .

History Skills. (2023, September 14). *The Valladolid Debate: When Europeans Argued About Whether Indigenous People Were Human.* Retrieved from Historyskills.com: HYPERLINK "https://www.historyskills.com/classroom/year-8/valladolid-debate/" https://www.historyskills.com/classroom/year-8/valladolid-debate/ .

History.com. (2023, June 27). *Amistad Case.* Retrieved from History.com: HYPERLINK "https://www.history.com/topics/slavery/amistad-case" https://www.history.com/topics/slavery/amistad-case .

Johnson, L. S. (2018, October 9). *Majorities in Sub-Saharan Africa Own Mobile Phones, But Smartphone Adoption Is Modest.* Retrieved from Pew Research Center: HYPERLINK "https://www.pewresearch.org/global/2018/10/09/majorities-in-sub-saharan-africa-own-mobile-phones-but-smartphone-adoption-is-modest/" https://www.pewresearch.org/global/2018/10/09/majorities-in-sub-saharan-africa-own-mobile-phones-but-smartphone-adoption-is-modest/ .

Lashmar, J. S. (2023, August 19). *A Huge Human Drama: How the Revolt That Began on the Gladstone Plantation Led to Emancipation.* Retrieved from Theguardian.com: HYPERLINK "https://www.theguardian.com/world/2023/aug/19/how-revolt-gladstone-plantation-led-to-emancipation-demerara-rebellion"
https://www.theguardian.com/world/2023/aug/19/how-revolt-gladstone-plantation-led-to-emancipation-demerara-rebellion .

LDHI. (2023, September 8). *Slavery before the Trans-Atlantic Trade.* Retrieved from Africn Passages, Lowcountry Adaptations: HYPERLINK "https://ldhi.library.cofc.edu/exhibits/show/africanpassageslowcountryadapt/introductionatlanticworld/slaverybeforetrade"
https://ldhi.library.cofc.edu/exhibits/show/africanpassageslowcountryadapt/introductionatlanticworld/slaverybeforetrade .

Liberte, Egalite, Fraternite. (2023, October 1). *The Code Noir (The Blak Code).* Retrieved from Revolution.chnm.org: HYPERLINK "https://revolution.chnm.org/d/335/" https://revolution.chnm.org/d/335/ .

Liberte, Egalite, raternte. (2023, October 1). *Slavery and the Haitian Revolution.* Retrieved from Revolution.chrm.org: HYPERLINK "https://revolution.chnm.org/exhibits/show/liberty--equality--fraternity/slavery-and-the-haitian-revolu" https://revolution.chnm.org/exhibits/show/liberty--equality--fraternity/slavery-and-the-haitian-revolu .

Lieblich, M. (2023, September 25). *The Cultural Significance of Solomon Northup's Twelve Years a Slave.* Retrieved from U.S. History Scene: HYPERLINK "https://ushistoryscene.com/article/12-years-a-slave/"
https://ushistoryscene.com/article/12-years-a-slave/ .

Lodi, C. (2023, September 18). *Washing of the Valongo Wharf, Rio de Janeiro (Brazil).* Retrieved from Whc.unesco.org: HYPERLINK "https://whc.unesco.org/en/canopy/valongo/"
https://whc.unesco.org/en/canopy/valongo/ .

Lyons, M. (2023, August). *The Valladolid Debate on the Rights of Indigenous People.* Retrieved from History Today: HYPERLINK "https://www.historytoday.com/archive/months-past/valladolid-debate-rights-indigenous-people" https://www.historytoday.com/archive/months-past/valladolid-debate-rights-indigenous-people .

Maroon History. (2023, October 1). *Maroon History.* Retrieved from Cyber.harvard.edu: HYPERLINK "https://cyber.harvard.edu/eon/marroon/history.html"
https://cyber.harvard.edu/eon/marroon/history.html .

Matthews, L. (2020, September 23). *Slavery in the Asante Empire of West Africa.* Retrieved from Mises.org: HYPERLINK "https://mises.org/mises-wire/slavery-asante-empire-west-africa" \l

":~:text=Asante%20society%20had%20numerous%20uses,as%20domestics%20 or%20farm%20laborers" https://mises.org/wire/slavery-asante-empire-west-africa#:~:text=Asante%20society%20had%20numerous%20uses,as%20domestics%20or%20farm%20laborers .

McKenna, A. (2023, September 8). *Dahomey.* Retrieved from Britannica.com: HYPERLINK "https://www.britannica.com/place/Dahomey-historical-kingdom-Africa" https://www.britannica.com/place/Dahomey-historical-kingdom-Africa .

Middle Passage Ceremonies and Port Markers Project (MPCPMP). (2012, January 11). *Personal Stories of Captured Africans.* Retrieved from Middle Passage Ceremonies and Port Markers Project (MPCPMP): HYPERLINK "https://www.middlepassageproject.org/2012/01/11/personal-stories-of-captured-africans/" https://www.middlepassageproject.org/2012/01/11/personal-stories-of-captured-africans/ .

Mitchell, R. (2023, April 10). *The Rise and Fall of Central Africa's Mighty Kingdom of Kongo.* Retrieved from Ancient Origins: HYPERLINK "https://www.ancient-origins.net/ancient-places-africa/kingdom-kongo-0018228" https://www.ancient-origins.net/ancient-places-africa/kingdom-kongo-0018228 .

Mohin, A. (2023, June 5). *Who Owns the Benin Bronzes? The Answer Just Got More Complicated.* Retrieved from NYTimes.com: HYPERLINK "https://www.nytimes.com/2023/06/04/arts/design/benin-bronzes-nigeria-ownership.html" https://www.nytimes.com/2023/06/04/arts/design/benin-bronzes-nigeria-ownership.html .

Momdou, S. (2017, August 13). *Bussa Rebellion (1816).* Retrieved from BlackPast: HYPERLINK "https://www.blackpast.org/global-african-history/bussa-rebellion-1816/" \l ":~:text=The%20rebellion%20took%20its%20name,by%20the%20British%20in%201838" https://www.blackpast.org/global-african-history/bussa-rebellion-1816/#:~:text=The%20rebellion%20took%20its%20name,by%20the%20British%20in%201838 .

Morris, G. (2017, July 1). *Unspeakable Cruelty: Former Slaves Tell Their Stories in Southern University Online Listings.* Retrieved from The Advocate: HYPERLINK "https://www.theadvocate.com/baton_rouge/entertainment_life/unspeakable-cruelty-former-slaves-tell-their-stories-in-southern-university-online-listings/article_996926ae-579c-11e7-9d36-13d23afca32d.html" https://www.theadvocate.com/baton_rouge/entertainment_life/unspeakable-cruelty-former-slaves-tell-their-stories-in-southern-university-online-listings/article_996926ae-579c-11e7-9d36-13d23afca32d.html .

Mrcaseyhistory. (2023, September 25). *King Afonso I, Letter to King John III of Portugal.* Retrieved from Mrcaseyhistory.files.wordpress.com:

HYPERLINK "https://mrcaseyhistory.files.wordpress.com/2014/05/king-afonso-i-letter-to-king-john-iii-of-portugal.pdf" https://mrcaseyhistory.files.wordpress.com/2014/05/king-afonso-i-letter-to-king-john-iii-of-portugal.pdf .

Msa.maryland.gov. (2023, September 30). *Thoughts upon Slavery.* Retrieved from Msa.maryland.gov: HYPERLINK "https://msa.maryland.gov/megafile/msa/speccol/sc5300/sc5339/000091/000000/000001/restricted/2002_09_10/wesley/thoughtsuponslavery.html" https://msa.maryland.gov/megafile/msa/speccol/sc5300/sc5339/000091/000000/000001/restricted/2002_09_10/wesley/thoughtsuponslavery.html .

National Park Service. (2023, September 17). *The Middle Passage.* Retrieved from Nps.gov: HYPERLINK "https://www.nps.gov/articles/the-middle-passage.htm" https://www.nps.gov/articles/the-middle-passage.htm .

National Humanities Center. (2023, September 18). *Slave Auctions.* Retrieved from Nationalhumanitiescener.org: HYPERLINK "https://nationalhumanitiescenter.org/pds/maai/enslavement/text2/slaveauctions.pdf" https://nationalhumanitiescenter.org/pds/maai/enslavement/text2/slaveauctions.pdf .

National Humanities Center. (2023, September 25). *Suicide among Slaves: A 'Very Last Resort.'* Retrieved from Nationalhumanitiesenter.org: HYPERLINK "https://nationalhumanitiescenter.org/pds/maai/emancipation/text2/suicide.pdf" https://nationalhumanitiescenter.org/pds/maai/emancipation/text2/suicide.pdf .

Nunn, N. (2017, February 27). *Understanding the Long-run Effects of Africa's Slave Trades.* Retrieved from cepr.org: HYPERLINK "https://cepr.org/voxeu/columns/understanding-long-run-effects-africas-slave-trades" https://cepr.org/voxeu/columns/understanding-long-run-effects-africas-slave-trades .

Papst, C. (2023, September 18). *At 13 Baltimore City High Schools, Zero Students Tested Proficient on 2023 State Math Exam.* Retrieved from Foxbaltimore.com: HYPERLINK "https://foxbaltimore.com/news/project-baltimore/at-13-baltimore-city-high-schools-zero-students-tested-proficient-on-2023-state-math-exam" https://foxbaltimore.com/news/project-baltimore/at-13-baltimore-city-high-schools-zero-students-tested-proficient-on-2023-state-math-exam .

Pasciuto, G. (2022, December 21). *7 Facts About the Kingdom of Kongo: Africa's Great Catholic State.* Retrieved from Thecollector.com: HYPERLINK "https://www.thecollector.com/kingdom-of-kongo-great-catholic-state/" https://www.thecollector.com/kingdom-of-kongo-great-catholic-state/ .

Pbs.org. (2023, September 8). *Confronting the Legacy of the African Slave Trade*. Retrieved from The Slave Kingdoms: HYPERLINK "http://www.pbs.org/wonders/Episodes/Epi3/slave_2.htm" http://www.pbs.org/wonders/Episodes/Epi3/slave_2.htm .

PBS.org. (2023, September 17). *Insurrection on Board a Slave Ship*. Retrieved from Pbs.org: HYPERLINK "https://www.pbs.org/wgbh/aia/part1/1h317.html" https://www.pbs.org/wgbh/aia/part1/1h317.html .

Pbs.org. (2023, September 30). *Race: The Power of an Illusion*. Retrieved from Pbs.org: HYPERLINK "https://www.pbs.org/race/000_About/002_04-background-02-03.htm" https://www.pbs.org/race/000_About/002_04-background-02-03.htm .

Polat, G. (2023, May 19). *Queen Nzinga: Badass African Queen That Fought the Portuguese & Won*. Retrieved from Trailblazing Women & LGBTQ Folks: HYPERLINK "https://letherfly.org/queen-nzinga-the-portuguese-sold-her-people-into-slavery-so-she-went-to-war/" https://letherfly.org/queen-nzinga-the-portuguese-sold-her-people-into-slavery-so-she-went-to-war/ .

Rediker, M. (2021, December 14). *The Transatlantic Slave Trade Ships: Trajectories of Death and Violence Across the Ocean*. Retrieved from Thefunambulist.net: HYPERLINK "https://thefunambulist.net/magazine/the-ocean/the-transatlantic-slave-trade-ships-trajectories-of-death-and-violence-across-the-ocean" https://thefunambulist.net/magazine/the-ocean/the-transatlantic-slave-trade-ships-trajectories-of-death-and-violence-across-the-ocean

Robin, C. (2015, May 12). *The Trials of Hannah Arendt*. Retrieved from The Nation: HYPERLINK "https://www.thenation.com/article/archive/trials-hannah-arendt/" https://www.thenation.com/article/archive/trials-hannah-arendt/

Rogers, K. (2020, April 30). *The Personal Stories of 3 Enslaved Africans, as Told by Their Bones*. Retrieved from Cnn.com: HYPERLINK "https://www.cnn.com/2020/04/30/world/enslaved-african-history-trans-atlantic-slave-trade-trnd-scn/index.html" https://www.cnn.com/2020/04/30/world/enslaved-african-history-trans-atlantic-slave-trade-trnd-scn/index.html .

Saylor.org. (2023, September 25). *The Kingdom of Dahomey*. Retrieved from The Transatlantic Slave Trade: HYPERLINK "https://learn.saylor.org/mod/book/view.php?id=54827&chapterid=40411" https://learn.saylor.org/mod/book/view.php?id=54827&chapterid=40411 .

Schama, S. (2006). *Rough Crossings*. New York, NY: HarperCollins Publishers.

Schaub, D. (1990, Fall). *Race and the Constitution*. Retrieved from National Affairs: HYPERLINK "https://www.nationalaffairs.com/public_interest/detail/race-and-the-constitution" https://www.nationalaffairs.com/public_interest/detail/race-and-the-constitution .

Sief, K. (2018, January 29). *An African Country Reckons with Its History of Selling Slaves.* Retrieved from Washington Post.com: HYPERLINK "https://www.washingtonpost.com/world/africa/an-african-country-reckons-with-its-history-of-selling-slaves/2018/01/29/5234f5aa-ff9a-11e7-86b9-8908743c79dd_story.html" https://www.washingtonpost.com/world/africa/an-african-country-reckons-with-its-history-of-selling-slaves/2018/01/29/5234f5aa-ff9a-11e7-86b9-8908743c79dd_story.html .

Slavery and Remembrance. (2023, September 14). *French Slave Trade.* Retrieved from Slaveryandremembrance.org: HYPERLINK "https://slaveryandremembrance.org/articles/article/?id=A0097" https://slaveryandremembrance.org/articles/article/?id=A0097 .

Slavery and Remembrance. (2023, September 17). *Middle Passage.* Retrieved from slaveryandremembrance.org: HYPERLINK "https://slaveryandremembrance.org/articles/article/?id=A0032" https://slaveryandremembrance.org/articles/article/?id=A0032 .

Slavery and Remembrance. (2023, September 17). *Slave Ship Mutinies.* Retrieved from Slaveryandremembrance.org: HYPERLINK "https://slaveryandremembrance.org/articles/article/?id=A0035" https://slaveryandremembrance.org/articles/article/?id=A0035 .

Slavery and Remembrance. (2023, September 14). *British Slave Trade.* Retrieved from Slaveryandremembrance.org: HYPERLINK "https://slaveryandremembrance.org/articles/article/?id=A0116" https://slaveryandremembrance.org/articles/article/?id=A0116 .

Slaveryandremembrance.org. (2023, September 8). *Oyo Empire.* Retrieved from Slaveryandremembrance.org: HYPERLINK "https://slaveryandremembrance.org/articles/article/?id=A0121" \l ":~:text=Enslaved%20laborers%20provided%20food%20for,and%20eventually%20ended%2C%20Oyo%20suffered" https://slaveryandremembrance.org/articles/article/?id=A0121#:~:text=Enslaved%20laborers%20provided%20food%20for,and%20eventually%20ended%2C%20Oyo%20suffered .

SLP. (2023, October 1). *Barbados Slave Code (1661-1667).* Retrieved from Slaverylawpower.org: HYPERLINK "https://slaverylawpower.org/barbados-slave-code/" https://slaverylawpower.org/barbados-slave-code/ .

Societe Generale. (2022, June 12). *From The CFA Franc To The eco, A Reform for the Convergence of West African Economics.* Retrieved from Societegenerale.com.

Steven J. Mitchell, e. a. (2020, July 23). *Genetic Consequences of the Transatlantic Slave Trade*. Retrieved from AJHG: HYPERLINK "https://www.cell.com/ajhg/fulltext/S0002-9297(20)30200-7" https://www.cell.com/ajhg/fulltext/S0002-9297(20)30200-7 .

Students of History. (2023, September 17). *The Triangle of Trade*. Retrieved from Studentsofhistory.com: HYPERLINK "https://www.studentsofhistory.com/the-triangle-of-trade" https://www.studentsofhistory.com/the-triangle-of-trade

Sutherland, C. (2007, July 16). *Haitian Revolution (1791-1804)*. Retrieved from BlackPast: HYPERLINK "https://www.blackpast.org/global-african-history/haitian-revolution-1791-1804/" https://www.blackpast.org/global-african-history/haitian-revolution-1791-1804/ .

Team, T. E. (2019, November 11). *The History of the Kingdom of Dahomey*. Retrieved from Blackhistorymonth.org: HYPERLINK "https://www.blackhistorymonth.org.uk/article/section/pre-colonial-history/the-history-of-the-kingdom-of-dahomey/" https://www.blackhistorymonth.org.uk/article/section/pre-colonial-history/the-history-of-the-kingdom-of-dahomey/ .

The Brazilian Report. (2020, May 13). *Slavery in Brazil*. Retrieved from Wilsoncenter.org: HYPERLINK "https://www.wilsoncenter.org/blog-post/slavery-brazil" https://www.wilsoncenter.org/blog-post/slavery-brazil .

The Gilder Lehrman Institute. (2023, September 17). *The Middle Passage, 1749*. Retrieved from Gilderlehman.org: HYPERLINK "https://www.gilderlehrman.org/history-resources/spotlight-primary-source/middle-passage-1749" https://www.gilderlehrman.org/history-resources/spotlight-primary-source/middle-passage-1749 .

The Guardian. (2023, September 30). *The Story of the Zong Slave Ship: A Mass Murder Masquerading as an Insurance Claim*. Retrieved from theguardian.com: HYPERLINK "https://www.theguardian.com/law/2021/jan/19/the-story-of-the-zong-slave-ship-a-mass-masquerading-as-an-insurance-claim" https://www.theguardian.com/law/2021/jan/19/the-story-of-the-zong-slave-ship-a-mass-masquerading-as-an-insurance-claim .

The History Press. (2023, September 30). *The Slavery Abolition Act of 1833*. Retrieved from Thehistorypress.co.uk: HYPERLINK "https://www.thehistorypress.co.uk/articles/the-slavery-abolition-act-of-1833/" https://www.thehistorypress.co.uk/articles/the-slavery-abolition-act-of-1833/ .

Thiebaut, R. (2023, April 26). *The WIC, The Dutch West India Company*. Retrieved from Projectmanifest.eu: HYPERLINK "https://www.projectmanifest.eu/the-wic-the-dutch-west-india-company-en-fr/" https://www.projectmanifest.eu/the-wic-the-dutch-west-india-company-en-fr/ .

Thothios.com. (2023, September 8). *The Causes and Effects of the Trans-Saharan Trade.* Retrieved from Thothios.com: HYPERLINK "https://www.thothios.com/c-1200-to-c-1450/unit-2-networks-of-exchange/trans-saharan-trade/" https://www.thothios.com/c-1200-to-c-1450/unit-2-networks-of-exchange/trans-saharan-trade/ .

UK Parliament. (2023, September 30). *Parliament Abolishes the Slave Trade.* Retrieved from Parliament.uk: HYPERLINK "https://www.parliament.uk/about/living-heritage/transformingsociety/tradeindustry/slavetrade/overview/parliament-abolishes-the-slave-trade/" https://www.parliament.uk/about/living-heritage/transformingsociety/tradeindustry/slavetrade/overview/parliament-abolishes-the-slave-trade/ .

US Equal Employment Opportunity Commission. (2023, September 30). *EEO-1 Data Collection.* Retrieved from Eeoc.gov: HYPERLINK "https://www.eeoc.gov/data/eeo-data-collections" \l ":~:text=The%20EEO%2D1%20Component%201,race%20or%20ethnicity%2C%20to%20the" https://www.eeoc.gov/data/eeo-1-data-collection#:~:text=The%20EEO%2D1%20Component%201,race%20or%20ethnicity%2C%20to%20the .

Ushistory.org. (2023, September 17). *The Middle Passage.* Retrieved from Ushistory.org: HYPERLINK "https://www.ushistory.org/us/6b.asp" https://www.ushistory.org/us/6b.asp .

Williams, F. G. (2023, September 14). *The Rise and Fall of Portugal's Maritime Empire, a Cautionary Tale?* Retrieved from Byustudies.byu.edu: HYPERLINK "https://byustudies.byu.edu/article/the-rise-and-fall-of-portugals-maritime-empire-a-cautionary-tale/" https://byustudies.byu.edu/article/the-rise-and-fall-of-portugals-maritime-empire-a-cautionary-tale/ .

Wiltz, A. (2023, April 19). *Are Creole People a Privileged or Oppressed, or Somewhere in Between?* Retrieved from Medium.com: HYPERLINK "https://medium.com/louisiana-creoles/are-creole-people-a-privileged-or-oppressed-or-somewhere-in-between-2f352a9882e" https://medium.com/louisiana-creoles/are-creole-people-a-privileged-or-oppressed-or-somewhere-in-between-2f352a9882e .

World History Commons. (2023, September 25). *Excerpt of Letter from Nzinga Mbemba to Portuguese King Jao III.* Retrieved from World History Commons: HYPERLINK "https://worldhistorycommons.org/excerpt-letter-nzinga-mbemba-portuguese-king-joao-iii" \l "doc_transcription" https://worldhistorycommons.org/excerpt-letter-nzinga-mbemba-portuguese-king-joao-iii#doc_transcription.

Zeeuwsarchief.ni. (2023, September 14). *The Voyage-History*. Retrieved from Zeeuwsarchief.ni: HYPERLINK "https://www.zeeuwsarchief.nl/en/themepage/slave-voyage-aboard-the-unity/the-voyage-history/" https://www.zeeuwsarchief.nl/en/themepage/slave-voyage-aboard-the-unity/the-voyage-history/ .

www.ingramcontent.com/pod-product-compliance
Lightning Source LLC
Chambersburg PA
CBHW070339010526
44107CB00004B/553